Praise for *Never Forget*

An Absolute Delight!

—Frieda Watt, author, The Displaced: Fall of a Fortress

A heroine after my own heart!

—Atiya Hussain, documentary film maker

Never Forget brings to life a dormant world in a captivating, unpredictable and timeless way.

—Samuelle Grove, photographer,
  Instagram: @samuellephotography

A fun romp through a really interesting part of Canadian history.

—Becca Madore

Well, Catherine, I just finished reading *Never Forget* and enjoyed it very much. I truly think you are our Canadian Jane Austin. I look forward to reading the second half.

—Aalia Hussain

A book that reminds us of the personal and everyday in history and the lives of those who lived it. The story explores universal struggles that are very relevant to today's climate.

—Amy Wood

Praise for *Never Forget*

Never Forget is an easy and enjoyable read. Being a historical novel, it carries one back in time to discover that human nature and the cultural, economic, and personal challenges Janet faced, remain today. Good work Catherine. A really good story.

—Joyce Hum, author/artist, christian outreach worker

Never Forget

by
Catherine Grove

Title: Never Forget
Format: Perfectbound book
ISBN: 978-1-9992393-0-5
Title: Never Forget (PDF)
Format: Ebook
ISBN: 978-1-9992393-1-2

Description: Janet Blythe defies family expectation and cultural norms to return to Regency England after the American War of 1812.

Cover photo: Samuelle Grove

Front cover design: Samuelle Grove (Instagram@samuellephotography)

Editor: Craig Macartney, Ottawa, Ontario

Design and Production: Budd Publishing, Ottawa, Ontario

Printed simultaneously in Canada and United States of America

To the readers I have yet to meet, thank you for joining me on this adventure.

To my sisters who sharpen me, my friends who bring out my best and my forthright children with their constructive criticism, thank you. And to Craig Macartney, Tim Kitz, Evelyn Budd and my supportive husband thank you for bringing Janet's story to print.

Never Forget
1814

Participants in order of appearance

Jane (Janet) Blythe

Nanny Wallace, Jane's caregiver as a child and chaperone as an adult

Reverend George Blythe (Papa to Jane), missionary at Elbema Falls

Sammy Smith and his mother, Martha

Captain Lord James Cliveton

Andrew Nettles, farmer at The Forty settlement

Soujeesh Stewart, Mohawk healer and Clan Mother

Mathew Hendrick and Simon, wounded sailors

Reverend and Mrs. Cameron and their many children

Captain Wesley Bryson, British Officer

Peter Cooper, British veteran

Lady Catherine Montbriar (nee Eldenmont)

Spencer Montbriar, deceased second son of Earl of Montbriar

Earl of Montbriar

Charles Eldenmont of Hurstmere (uncle of Jane Blythe,
    brother of Lady Catherine Montbriar)

Lady Charlotte Fairworth Eldenmont (wife of Charles)

    sister: Lady Olivia Fairworth

    daughters: Miss Daphnia Eldenmont and Miss Abigail Eldenmont

Mr. William Garnett, widower from Cornwall

Daniel Fremont, Heir to Hurstmere

Nicolas Fairworth, Earl of Albyne (stepbrother of Charlotte and Olivia,
    husband to Elspeth Pinney)

Mr. and Mrs. Pinney

    daughters: Sylvia Pinney and Elspeth Pinney Fairworth

Reverend and Mrs. Haynes of the Mariners Mission, London

Preface

The lay of the land

Eighteen colonies formed British North America until 1776. That year, 13 colonies broke away to form the United States of America. They called themselves the Patriots and waged eight years of war for independence. At first it was viewed as a civil war. Americans, who remained fiercely loyal to the Crown, were known as Loyalists. The Patriots called themselves Republicans.

In the black-and-white world of revolution, those loyal to the Crown and its parliamentary system were soon considered traitors to this new Republic. Persecuted by vicious mobs, their property was seized and legal rights denied. They sought refuge from the prevailing Republicans in the loyal Canadian colonies to the north, in the West Indies, or by returning to Britain.

The British imposed restrictive proclamations and treaties on the fledging Republic to undermine its economy and limit access to international trade. Since slavery was essential to commerce, the Philipsburg Proclamation of 1779 freed, armed and granted land in the Canadian colonies to all the slaves of revolutionaries who declared loyalty to the Monarchy. No such offer was extended to the Loyalists' slaves.

With the Quebec Act of 1774, the British supported resistance of the Iroquois Six Nations to westward expansion into the backcountry of the Appalachian Mountains. The Act also extended Aboriginal land rights south of the Great Lakes between the Ohio and Mississippi Rivers. Britain guaranteed freedom of Catholic faith, language and civil law for French Canadians of the Quebec colony to ensure loyalty against northward expansion of the Republic.

The western frontier of the British Great Lakes opened up. What followed was an orderly mixture of exception and inconsistency, as American and Mohawk refugees populated this Upper Canada. Diverse Loyalists found refuge among Indigenous people, British fortune seekers and French Canadians of the centuries-old colony. The new colony accommodated Roman Catholic rights, landowning-African freemen working alongside Loyalists' slaves, and Mohawk warriors living among hardened American veterans from an earlier French-Indian war.

From 1805 to 1815, Napoleon attempted domination of Europe to bring economic stability out of the French revolution. Britain fought back, seizing American ships and crews to prevent trade and support of France. A retaliatory war played out in the Canadian frontier between the American Republic and the British colonies. Patriots presumed all they had to do was to march in and proclaim these northern colonies free of British Rule. Kentucky frontiersmen invaded the Niagara Peninsula. New Englanders surged north to free the French Canadians. American and British naval ships engaged on the interior Great Lakes and tributaries.

Yet, the "mob rule" carnage of the American Republic's birth was not forgotten. The Aboriginal confederacy, former slaves, veterans of the Independence War and local militia united with British Regulars and Navy to resist the many attempts at invasion. They refused to capitulate, despite being outnumbered seven to one, having their parliament burned to the ground, and the battlefield deaths of two great leaders: the British Major-General Sir Isaac Brock and Tecumseh, the Aboriginal. This peculiar Canadian diversity persevered for the common good.

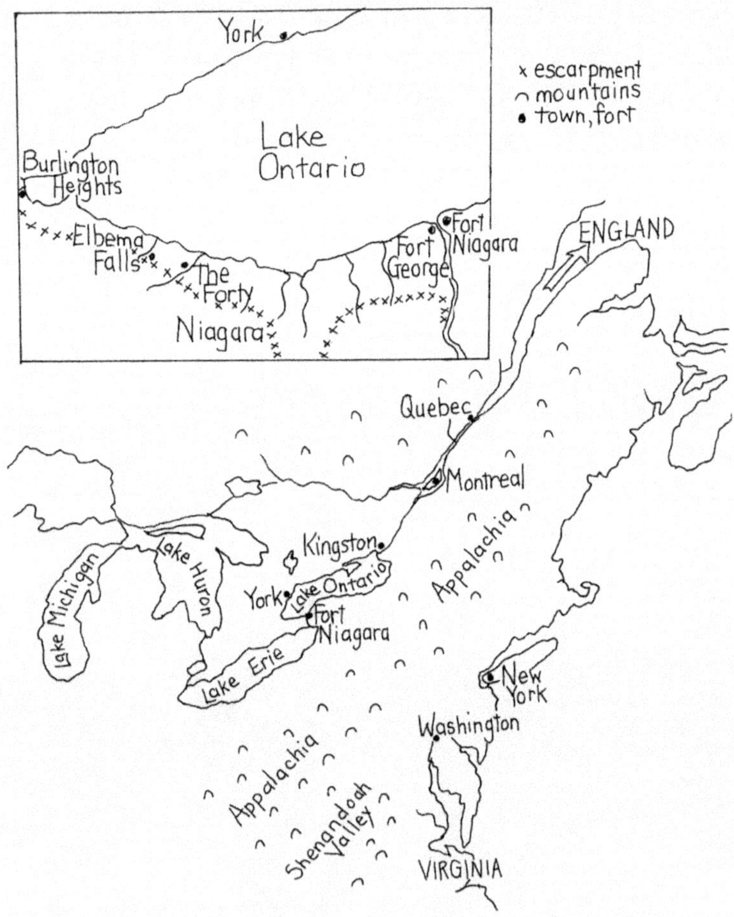

Map 1: Northeastern American

Map 2: England

Never Forget

Part I An Acorn Falls

Chapters 1–11

Part II Away from the Oak

Chapters 12–23

Love alters not with his brief hours and weeks,
But bears it out even to the edge of doom.

William Shakespeare, Sonnet 116

Part I An Acorn Falls

Chapter 1

The Niagara Frontier, March 1814.

A lone cannon fired out over the dark lake. The echo rumbled off the surrounding cliffs, rolling on into silence.

I hoped it was just a warning shot. Nanny woke with a sharp snort.

"Do you think it's an engagement?" I snuggled into her plump warm body.

A second shot answered for her, its timber louder and deeper. Two ships were out there, both near to shore. With ice breakup, the Americans had returned.

"Appears to be," she murmured.

Last summer, the Americans had occupied the entire western shore of Lake Ontario. They had camped just south of us, lobbing heated shot at British ships. Eventually, strengthened by British and Mohawk warriors, militiamen from The Forty settlement, drove them south to Fort

George. Burlington Heights must be their intended destination this time, I thought. They certainly weren't interested in us. Little of value remained at our mission outpost after that last occupation—except glass windowpanes and Papa's books.

We waited in silence. After a time, I slipped from under the covers to see what I could. Scratching off a corner of the frost that coated the windowpane, I peered through. The sky was overcast, but enough light reflected off the snow to see about. No flames were visible at The Forty so I knew they weren't under fire. Andrew Nettles' house was safe. It might have become my home, had I been more obliging and he a bit more accepting.

"Only two ships out on the lake," I concluded.

"Back to bed, lass," Nanny mumbled. "They're not interested in us."

Flittering caught my eye, just as I turned away from the window. Something scurried across the backdrop of snow, over in the graveyard. It was too large for a rabbit or raccoon. Maybe it was a deer.

I scanned the yard anticipating more movement, but was soon distracted by a volley of cannon, which cast eerie flickering light on the five crosses nearest the gate. These marked the graves of bodies washed up on the beach—men known only to God. It seemed as if they were crying out to be claimed. Papa, my mother and infant brother were out there too, in peaceful rest.

"Love alters not," I whispered the near-faded inscription on my mother's monument. Only three words fit on her cross, along with her name and years. The wise words warned me to not change those I loved into what I wanted them to be.

I snickered to myself. The words came from a Shakespeare verse, "Love alter not with his brief hours and weeks, but bears it out even to the edge of doom." Shakespeare wrote of love's constancy, even beyond death, though I thought of it as referring to love as an agent and not a sentiment. My simple interpretation helped when Andrew tried to mold me into another. This wasn't love.

The night tore open with a gut-kicking blast. A second followed right after, with equal fury. Echoes caught me in a frantic embrace. Flames rained down on one of the ships, igniting a sail. The growing flames now exposed the silhouette of the other ship. They lunged at each other merging in macabre dance. My stomach lurched. To tell friend from foe in such frenzy was not possible.

Screams traveled across the water, the cries of men fighting for life and the agony of those dying. "Dear God, make good come out of this," I silently prayed. The barrage carried on only a few minutes before fading to sporadic outbursts. Lake battles rarely lasted long— better to beat a hasty retreat than lose the ship.

The night fell silent again. Nanny's snoring resumed. I stayed at the window, watching for a landing party. Dear God, make them sail off into the night and leave us alone.

African refugees were never safe in this war. Martha Smith slept in Papa's old room across the hall and Sammy on a cot in the kitchen. They had come to us just before winter set in, refugees from the Shenandoah. I could hear

Sammy stirring, below. Footsteps slowly creaked up the wooden stairs to our rooms. They were heavier than when he had first come. He'd grown over the winter. Though only ten years old, he was almost the size of a man.

He rapped on his mother's door. "You all right, Mama?"

"Go back to bed, my sweet," she soothed. "It's over for now." He retreated to the kitchen.

I slipped my filleting knife under my pillow. It did me no good in my boot under the bed.

I woke to Sammy's soft rap at our door. The room was still dark.

Nanny gently poked an elbow into my side. "Get up and beat those foxes to the traps, Janet."

Only Nanny called me Janet. To Papa I'd always been Jane.

I slipped out from the quilts and into my wool trousers. Even through thick wool socks the floor felt cold. Tucking in my nightshirt, I pulled on my mukluks, and slid my knife down the outside of my right boot. The kitchen fire was already rekindled when I got down. Sammy was waiting for me, wearing Papa's bearskin overcoat. It fit him better than me. My buckskin coat had become loose over the winter, but would be warm enough with felt mitts and a wool tuque.

Snowshoes were no longer needed this late in winter. Though an early thaw, a few weeks back, had teased us into thinking spring had come, a numbing cold still held us tight and the ground remained frozen. Out on the lake, the rising sun was only a faint glow in the thick fog. Today would be warm; fog was a sure sign.

Whatever had lurked in the cemetery would be sure to be looking for a meal—just like us. With any luck it was a turkey. My mouth began to water at the thought of turkey, roasting on a spit. Maybe it was already snagged in one of our snares. If not, with my bow we would surely get something.

We tramped a short distance south along Mohawk Path, before climbing down into the creek bed. Silently we continued toward the lakeshore. Sound travels easily in cold fog. We didn't want to scare off our prey.

The snares were empty, but I found a stash of acorns left in a stump hollow by a forgetful squirrel. They had a musty odor, but once roasted they would be fit to eat. I stuffed my pouch full.

Sammy scampered back up the bank to check the snares on the ridge. I continued to the lake. All was quiet and the water still. Gruesome evidence from last night's combat would eventually wash up. Today's thick fog made looking for any flotsam a waste of effort. Tomorrow I'll give the shoreline a look over.

"Hey!" Sammy shouted from above.

I looked up. He held high a limp rabbit. The poor scrawny creature had survived the winter only to end up in our cooking pot. Whatever had caught my eye in the graveyard last night must have evaded our snares, at least for now. I scrambled up the icy rocks to meet him. Clods of earth broke away from the thawing bank, cascading with noisy splashes below. Whipping out my knife, I sliced off an ear and tucked it between the branches of the nearest bush.

"Why do you always do that?" he asked.

"To honor him for giving his life," I answered. "I'll thank God, tonight, when we eat him."

My neck tingled. I looked behind, half-expecting something to jump out from the bushes. Nothing was there. Neither was anything visible down along the shore. I held my breath and listened. Something was out there; the sensation was real.

I waited. The lake was calm. Amidst those few random waves sloshing against the rock I could make out a shout of "Give Way!" followed by "Backwater," and again "Give Way!" which could only be boat commands. A longboat pierced through the fog, towards us. Its Union Jack hung limp from a central mast. Eight oars lifted. I pulled Sammy to the ground.

"It's British, not American," he protested, confused. "We're safe, Jane."

"Not if they want to press us to serve their ship." I had other troubles to add to this threat should they discover I was a maid in trousers.

A musket lifted up and a deep voice growled, "Who goes there?" I rose up, arms held high, to show I was unarmed. Amid the oarsmen, another occupant was visible in the boat, wrapped in a shroud and readied on a pallet for burial.

"Identify yourself!" The captain stood at the head of the boat. An American sharpshooter could easily pick him off in that Royal Navy bicorn hat.

"God save the King!" I called out in my huskiest voice. "Blythe is my name, sir, of the Elbema Falls Mission. Our landing is yonder, that large flat rock. I'll draw you ashore."

We raced to meet the boat as it pulled up. "Ship Oars," ordered the lead oarsman, followed by "Rack Oars". The captain tossed me the rope and leapt ashore, a man no more than thirty, not yet weathered by life on the open sea. He bore the same gravity I'd seen in other British officers during this war.

I knotted the rope around the sturdy stump, under his scrutiny. Even after I stood to meet his wolf-like eyes he continued to study me. With a frown, he turned his gaze to our surroundings before settling on Sammy.

"Sammy Smith is a loyal British subject, you can be assured," I stepped between them.

"Does he not speak for himself?" the officer snapped.

"You've come to bury your dead," I returned, attempting to regain his attention.

"I thought the mission abandoned." He looked up the path towards the chapel. The log steeple was faintly visible through the fog.

"Not all of us fled," I answered unable to suppress the edge in my voice.

He returned to study me. That was when I noticed his eyes were grey.

"I shall leave four to your care," he pronounced.

"Not without supplies, sir!" I hurled back. "We can't possibly take them without provisions. Surely you have a surgeon aboard your ship? Can they not be sent on to Fort George?"

"You will get what you need." He turned to the longboat crew and directed them ashore. Conscripted to their care, I knew replacement for both the dead and the wounded would be needed. Sammy had to get away.

"I will send for Soujeesh, the healer. Her village is nearby." It was the first thing that came to mind to get Sammy away. I didn't know if she was even up there.

"An Indian woman?" the captain exclaimed.

I took this as insult. "You're fortunate someone so skilled is close enough to help! She served under Tecumseh in the Battle on the Thames."

"We were defeated at the Thames." His jaw clenched, inviting challenge.

"You can't fault her for that, sir. We were outnumbered and Tecumseh died there, loyal to the British crown."

His features softened. "That he did." He nodded in vague assent. "What does it matter who does the healing if limb or life might be saved? As it is, they'll likely not survive."

I took the rabbit from Sammy and whispered for him to remain at the village until the ship left. Without waiting for leave, he bolted up the path, continued past the mission and onto the escarpment trail.

The slight, swaddled form on the pallet suggested the dead sailor had been young, probably little older than Sammy. Gingerly the tired bearers lifted him up the icy bank, taking care not to slip and stumble. It would be sad to drop their precious load. It would be even sadder, if I didn't get the supplies needed to care for those still alive.

With a command of "Oars Off," the four remaining oarsmen steadied to push off. I needed to ensure we got those provisions.

"Sir!" My protest came out shrill with tension.

"Good Lord! What now?" He turned on me with a growl.

"Supplies, sir." I held up the lifeless rabbit. "This bit of bones and fur, and a few moldy acorns, are all I have to feed your men. We've nothing at the mission for ourselves."

"The men I leave are beyond need of food." He spoke slowly, infused with anger. "Be useful and take us to that burial ground."

"So would you have them starve to death?" I stood my ground, angered by his disregard for our needs. "Is this how the British care for those who serve?"

"I'm leaving them to die," he snarled, eyes flashing. "You'll get what is needed. Just…" He raised his hand.

I crouched anticipating the blow. Our eyes engaged.

"Just go." He flicked his hand, as if I were an annoying gnat.

"We must have a crock of strong drink," I demanded, thinking of its need for pain.

Disgust filled his face and he turned to give final direction to the lead oarsman. Likely he thought I was going to drink it.

"Where's your decency?" I shouted at his back. "Think about their suffering! Pain alone can kill if we must amputate or set bones."

He ordered the boat away. I tore up to the vicarage without waiting for dismissal. A gravelly voice bellowed after me to start digging, but was cut short by a command from the captain, "Silence!"

Nanny and Martha started to their feet when I burst into the cabin.

"What's amiss, lass?" Nanny took the rabbit and firmly shut the door.

"A British ship has landed." I spilled the acorns out onto the table. "A burial party," I added breathlessly.

"Were you seen like that?" she huffed.

I groaned at her familiar fuming over respectability. "Papa never minded trousers, and we've far more to worry about than my—"

"Mind your cheek!" she snapped. "Your Papa's no longer here to stand for you!"

"Where's my Sammy?" Martha interrupted, grasping her son's danger.

I assured her he was safe up the escarpment on his way to the Mohawk village.

"We need to make ready for casualties from last night's battle and prepare at least one grave. And I did my best to argue for provisions," I concluded.

"I'll fetch hot coals to thaw the ground and show them where to dig." Nanny shifted attention to the necessary preparation. "Martha will ready the chapel for those poor lads. And you can start a soup, Janet. We'll share what we can—and you're nae part of it!" She ordered me first to put on something decent.

I bowed my head in feigned contriteness. Before going up, I fetched the charity basket of knitted items from under the stair and set it by the door. These were items made over the winter to give refugees passing through. Those sailors also could do with this bit of consideration. Upstairs I threw my brown dress over my clothes and wrapped my mother's green shawl about my shoulders. I tied my unbraided hair about my face. Hopefully this would lose any semblance to the lad who had tied their boat at the landing.

Chapter 2

Down from my room, I rushed to find Nanny kneeling at the bottom of the stairs, sorting out spare bedding from the storage trunk. Last night had been cold. I didn't mind giving away knitted items, but I wasn't so generous about our quilts.

"Fire's lit in the chapel brazier." She looked up with a hard stare. "Martha and I will wash the wounded while you wait for Soujeesh. And mind—"

Without waiting for her to finish, I turned the corner to the kitchen, running smack into Andrew Nettles.

"Whoa, little lady. Slow down." He grasped my shoulders possessively.

A shiver shot up my spine at his touch. I stepped back and he loosened his grip.

"Don't worry, Jane. I've only come to warn you that an American has been seen lurking around these parts, the past few days. But then," he smirked. "I shouldn't worry about you, aye? He's probably already known at the mission."

Our eyes locked. Long ago I learned that ignoring his provocation irked him far more than any argument. Martha's chopping knife quickened at the table behind us. Andrew glanced back at her, annoyed.

"I've written the mission board about your father's replacement. I've also requested a teaching position for you—perhaps in a welcoming place like York."

He paused in anticipation of my appreciation. I said nothing. Nanny sniffed.

"All in Christian love, aye?" he concluded. "Pray, remember my home is always open should you have need."

I would sooner starve, I thought, biting my tongue. That was when I noticed the captain watching from the hearth. He had come in while I was upstairs.

Andrew turned to the captain.

"We'll see you soon at The Forty, sir. Until then, may good fortune follow you!"

With an abrupt farewell he left. Through the open door I could see the new grave was nearly dug.

"Mr. Nettles has forgotten his manners," Martha muttered, while fastening her apron around my waist. Gently, she directed me to the hearth.

"You've not been properly introduced, Captain Cliveton, to Miss Jane Blythe and her guardian, Mrs. Wallace."

He bowed curtly to us then asked, "And you are?"

She answered promptly, took an armful of linen from Nanny and they left for the chapel. Alone with the captain, I returned to the table and gave full attention to soup preparation.

16

"Pray, forgive my rudeness," he tendered in a contrite tone. "I hadn't realized that you are George Blythe's daughter. I am James Cliveton, Captain of the HMS *Dominion*."

I made no response, but worked the rolling pin over the nuts with far more force than needed. I was still rankled by Andrew and had no desire to converse with this man.

"For the apparel oft proclaims the man," he orated, loud enough to not be ignored.

Matching his volume, I recited:

> To thine own self be true,
> And it must follow, as night the day,
> Thou canst not then be false to any man.

He coughed—whether stifling a laugh or fighting a grippe, I wasn't sure.

"The Bard of Avon was my father's favorite escape." I delivered him a hard stare. "So is it my clothes or simply me you mock?" I resumed rolling bits of meat in the nut meal.

"I mean no disrespect, Miss Blythe." His pleasant smile bore little resemblance to the stern captain of the landing. "I just wasn't expecting Hamlet from a woman in buckskins, on the Niagara frontier. You are a welcome reprieve."

"I dress out of need and not in masquerade." I waved my rolling pin at his heavy Naval overcoat and the bicorn hat on his lap. "That's more than can be said about your kit."

He set the hat on the floor under the chair. I joined him by the fire, hung a cauldron of water to boil and began browning the meat and nuts in a skillet. From his breast pocket he drew out a handkerchief and blew his nose. He watched me without saying another word. As the flames continued their dance, his head sank towards his chest and his eyes glazed over.

"Are you ailing, Captain?" I conceded, suspecting he had fallen asleep, eyes open.

He shook his head with an abrupt sniff. "Rarely 'm I sat in-a kitch'n," he slurred.

"Perhaps you would prefer my father's study? There's no fire, but—"

"Heavens, no!" he sputtered, now fully awake. "This is very agreeable."

I scraped the browned meat and skillet drippings into the simmering cauldron, and sprinkled in dried sage and thyme.

"Stay as long as you like." I sat across from him on a stool.

"What do you mean about my naval issue?" He leaned back in the chair, crossing his arms, and looked at me with a raised eyebrow.

"You have to pay for it yourself, don't you? From what I can see it a bad bargain. That bicorn hat is useless protection against winter's bite. Your nose and ears are red, runny and probably aching."

"And I'm not handsome to start—" He stretched his hands towards the fire. "I must look a right fright."

I laughed. He didn't.

"Handsomeness is a gift of birth, sir. Attractiveness is a work of character," I offered in encouragement.

He smiled at the fire.

"I'll give you a proper tuque, scarf, mittens and pair of thick socks when you go out. If you keep head and ears warm, the body will stay warm too."

"My image will suffer." He yawned.

"It will be quite some image if your nose and toes rot off with frost's bite."

He burst into hearty vibrant laughter. "Then my character will surely need even more work."

A spark flew from the fire. He stomped it out. "You are refreshing, Miss Blythe. I know you intended no harm at the landing, but pray take care how you speak. A less tolerant person might take your comments as rebellious to the Crown."

"How can you fancy yourself tolerant, sir, if you think it treasonous to defend men who serve the Crown? Surely you must agree they deserve respect?"

"My opinion is of no concern." He sat up straight, rubbing his eyes.

"Then I will say my piece, Captain, just so there's no misunderstanding of mine. During the occupation, last year, the American army confiscated my musket and horse, ate most of my chickens, but left my milk cow alone. When the British liberated us, they butchered my cow and ate her right out there in my yard, along with my remaining chickens. You treated us worse than our enemies. Is that just reward for loyalty?"

"Were you not fairly compensated for what we took?" He looked at me intently.

"I was given money, aye, but where's another cow to be bought these days?" I leaned over to stir the soup. "And this isn't just about cheese or butter, sir. I grew molds in that milk—"

Voices outside captured his attention.

"I must go," he reached for his hat under the chair. "My men have come with your supplies." He stood up to fasten his overcoat.

"What is the name of the lad we bury?" I followed him to the door. "When the weather warms, I'll mark the grave."

"Tom Haddon, of Sussex," he replied. "He was barely 16 years on the earth."

I pushed a navy scarf and tuque into his hands. Both matched his uniform. "You need protection in this cold, Captain."

He slipped the hat into his pocket and wrapped the scarf about his neck, tucking it under his overcoat.

"Be assured we are on the same side," I offered to dispel any suspicion planted by either my or Andrew's comments.

"And what side might that be, Miss Blythe?" His challenge seemed half in jest, half in contemplation.

"The side that seeks justice and opportunity for all," I answered.

The door flew open and Nanny came in to announce the chapel was ready for the casualties.

Chapter 3

The sailors brought in generous supplies of wheat, sugar, cheese, oil, smoked hams, apples, turnips, onions and a cage with two hens. With a bow and a quick touch to their forelock, they left me to blend up bread and scones. The bread would rise and scones bake while I attended the burial.

With my mother's shawl about me, and my head uncovered, I went out to the cemetery. Captain Cliveton motioned me into the circle of men gathered around the open grave. He opened the Book of Common Prayer of the Church of England and began to read the Service for the Burial of the Dead. His intonations and gestures were both sober and sincere. Unrushed, he paused frequently to ensure engagement of all. At the final "Adieu" I could not doubt his reverence. Before laying the corpse in, he invited his crew for further observation, if they desired.

A raw wind whipped around us, stirring up icy bits of dirt. Men shuffled, hesitant and unsure. I sensed something further was needed. As always, fear hovered. This was war and men never knew when their time would come. I wanted to encourage them through this final farewell. One of Papa's favorite choruses came to mind: "O Waly, Waly". I closed my eyes and began to sing.

> A ship there is, and she sails the sea,
> She's loaded deep, as deep can be,
> But not so deep as the love I'm in,
> I know not if I sink or swim.

Raspy voices soon joined me in the familiar song.

> I leaned my back against an oak,
> Thinkin' it was a trusty tree,
> But first it bent and then it broke,
> So did my love prove false to me.

I opened my eyes as the swaddled body lowered into the ground. Ropes that held him to the living were being let go.

> Must I go bound while you go free,
> Must I love a man who doesn't love me,
> Must I be born with so little art,
> As to love a man who'll break my heart.

Across from me, an old sailor dug into the pile of earth and tossed it into the grave. The dull thud was like a closing door. He passed the shovel to the next man and each took his turn until Tom Haddon was buried deep.

> When cockleshells turn silver bells,
> Then will my love come back to me,
> When roses bloom in winter's gloom,
> Then will my love return to me.

The captain remained apart from the others, away from the grave, his face rigid. If he was offended—so be it. I had no regret for singing this song. I only knew that from this day forward, whenever it was sung, Tom would again be among his comrades.

> The water is wide, I cannot cross o'er,
> Neither have I the wings to fly,
> Give me a boat that can carry two,
> And both shall row, my love and I.

Nanny and Martha stayed in the chapel, caring for the wounded men. The Captain had said they were beyond hope; in that case there was no need to hurry. These sailors around the grave also needed care, for some bore burns and gashes from last night's combat. A large fire had been built at the center of the barnyard and they gathered about it, attempting to stay warm. Likely many served against their will, pressed into service or as an alternative to prison. Had Sammy not escaped up the mountain, he might have been pressed to join them.

From the kitchen, I retrieved salves and bandages to treat their injuries. I also brought a basket of warm scones, slices of ham, mugs, and a bucket of healing tea. I could not begrudge them this comfort. Neither could I deny their request for another song.

"Of all the comrades that e'er I had," I launched into another of Papa's favorite ballads. "They're sorry for my going away..."

That was all that was needed to spark their impromptu wake. I returned to the cabin to await Soujeesh. The captain had resumed his place by the kitchen hearth. His liberty strangely warmed me.

"That ham was for your sole use, Miss Blythe. You needn't feed my men." His voice was warm and he asked if he might also have some of the tea I had served his men.

"Those men have had a difficult go—as we all have." I prepared him a mug.

He sniffed the contents and frowned like a curious child.

"It will fight off infection," I coaxed, "or at least strengthen you. It's brewed from spruce bark and I've added a few herbs for flavor."

He nodded and drank. Then he accepted a bowl of soup, with a scone.

"I found your prayers encouraging, Captain Cliveton." I bit into my scone hungrily, risking later vomiting, for surgery always upset my stomach.

"You would be a connoisseur of such business, I imagine. Your late father was respected for his work among the Native peoples. But Miss Blythe—would tavern songs please him?"

"That ballad was a favorite of my father's and most suitable—"

"Then you don't fall far from the oak."

I let the comment pass and asked if he expected more engagement with the Americans that night.

"Not likely, so don't fear. They fared much worse." He dunked the scone into his soup, stuffing it into his mouth.

"I'm not afraid." I passed him another and finished mine. "Just weary from three years of humiliating scheming."

"I admire your shrewdness, Miss Blythe. And be assured my men will treat you with the upmost respect, after you've been so kind."

"Would I fare as well if I were African, Native or not so kind?"

"No." He set his empty bowl on the floor.

"Should not all who serve the Crown deserve justice?"

"Justice is an illusion," he answered quietly. "Our king is mad. The Regent is a rake who chooses to play instead of lead." He stabbed a finger in the direction of the cemetery. "And that lad—" He faltered, and drew a deep breath. "That lad was full of life, yesterday, and now he's planted with four more soon to join him." Abruptly he shook his head, as if astonished by this admission.

I certainly was.

With a shrug and a flash of his teeth, our eyes met. "I blather on, Miss Blythe. Pray, forget my nonsense."

A blast of cold air flooded the room before I could assure him. Soujeesh stomped in with a firm slam of the cabin door.

"Ah-ha! Something smells delicious!" she exclaimed in Mohawk. Then, fixing on the captain. "And someone looks delicious!"

"You speak Mohawk?" He looked surprised. I felt sure that he had caught my blush.

"Take me to your wounded," Soujeesh said, switching to English.

It was only mid-day. The sky remained overcast and a light fog remained. She had slipped by the sailors without their notice. Crossing back across the yard they broke off from singing and leapt to their feet. The captain stopped to speak to them before following us into the chapel.

A small brazier fire bathed the log chapel in gentle light. The men were settled on pallet beds. I lifted my hands in silent anticipation. *May my hands be Yours, O Lord.*

"There's a good lass." Nanny looked up from a still form. "Have a look at this one while I go fetch more boiled water. Mathew Hendrick is the lad's name."

I stroked his matted hair. "We've come to tend to your wounds, Mathew," I whispered.

His eyes fluttered open and he looked up at me. His implicit trust saddened my heart. *Please God, may mine not be the last face he sees on this Earth!*

Gently I lifted the covering over his legs. He whimpered in agony.

"Oh Lord, have mercy!" The words slipped out at the sight of the bloody pulp of muscle and bone that had once been a leg. All definition was destroyed below the knee. Only the crushing of tissue had saved his life by stopping the flow of blood.

Youthful strength had kept him so far. I could only hope it would continue to do so. If his heart endured the amputation, we would battle putrefaction over the coming days. I manipulated the other leg. He shrieked at my touch. Mercifully the break of bone was clean. It would heal and support him, should he survive the amputation. Only he could choose if this was to be a blessing or a curse.

"Christ have mercy," he moaned in ritualized prayer response. The poor man was still aware of his circumstances.

"And He will." I covered his leg and directed Martha to give him a cup of whiskey.

The captain stepped out from the shadows, wide-eyed with horror. Until then I don't think he realized that I was to assist Soujeesh.

"We must remove his lower leg," Soujeesh declared calmly in Mohawk. Using her native tongue allowed us free discussion around those we worked on.

"Can you leave enough for a peg?" I asked.

"I will try," she sighed. "And you will do what you can with the other leg so he can again stand."

The captain knelt next to us and pulled back the covering.

"Is this any work for a woman?" he whispered.

"Does it matter who does the healing if limb or life be saved?" I repeated his earlier words. "We will do what we can, sir. Pray, invite in two capable men to restrain him should he stay alert."

He left and we completed our assessment of the others. The shattered right arm of the man called Simon would have to be removed. Martha impelled him to drink enough whiskey to bring on stupor—it would mute both pain and fear. He accepted. The remaining two men were beyond help, barely breathing. Perhaps this was a mercy.

One had a large piece of wooden shrapnel impaled in his bowels; his life oozing away. The other was badly burned; I was amazed he had survived this long.

"I'll sit with them until their time," Nanny offered reverently.

Soujeesh readied her knife, saw and cauterizing iron in the brazier coals. Nanny's quiet singing of a lullaby calmed the room and brought me comfort as two sailors entered, summoned by the captain. I directed them to take hold of Mathew and placed a smooth slat of wood between his teeth, ordering him to bite down.

Mercifully he passed out as we began to work on him, making both the surgery and setting of his remaining leg easier. After Mathew, we worked on Simon, then there was nothing to do but wait.

Hours passed into evening. Both survived amputation. The other two men quietly slipped into eternity. Nanny and Martha sewed them into a sailcloth shroud, ready for burial. Our assistants from the ship began two graves before leaving. The ground was frozen and the hour too late for them to finish. Martha and I would do our best in the morning.

Soujeesh and I slipped out for a brief refreshment. Martha and Nanny had already gone to bed. All was quiet in our cabin. On the table waited a loaf of bread, a generous wedge of cheese and a flask that I assumed to be from the captain's private wine. Next to these I found a document bearing a crimson seal, embedded with a *D*, signed by Captain Cliveton. He'd written a commendation for "Master Samuel Smith," in appreciation of his assistance to the Crown. This would be invaluable to Martha and her son when claiming a land allotment.

"You're growing in strength, my Jane. You did not hold back this time." Soujeesh filled my goblet with wine. "And your stomach held, too!"

Images of the surgeries still flooded my mind. Sensing my struggle, she squeezed my hand. "Someday you will see beyond the person, into the healing."

We sat in silence. Tension eased as the wine took hold.

"I will sleep in the chapel," she yawned. "Should I have need, I'll ring the bell." She nodded towards the lake. "That man is worthy of you."

"The Captain?" I was surprised at her approval. "Even though he's a Britisher?"

"Worthy men are never limited by birth. Look at your Papa." Her face softened with a smile. "And my Johnnie, of course. In the forty years since those Americans felled him I've not wanted another."

Whenever wine loosened her tongue she would speak of her husband. I much preferred that than when she spoke of the British. Tonight I was spared neither.

"We Mohawk live at the mercy of those damned British." She clenched her teeth, emitting a sound as though she had been stung. "While they want nothing of our ways, they'll have us do their butchery. We are protected as long as they have use for us. What will they do when that day ends?"

I didn't answer. My thoughts drifted to Papa. He sent me to her when I was 15 to learn herbal medicine and bone setting. For two years I lived among her people, acquiring their language and their ways. Although Mohawk women did most of the labor, they also held rights to land, leadership and had a voice equal to men on the tribal council. Papa admired this, for it agreed with his vision of equality between men and woman in the Kingdom of God.

"You are a leader." Soujeesh pierced my thoughts. "Don't ever forget this, even when your people deny you a proper place." With a condescending snort she rapped her knuckles on the table. "Promise me that you will never join with a man who holds you with disdain."

"Of course, Grandmother," I reassured her, as always. My curiosity remained piqued for she seldom spoke well of any European. "How can you say this captain is worthy of me when you saw so little of him."

"He trusted us to our work—that is rare for a Britisher." She held up her empty goblet and cackled, "And his wine is good."

"He'd likely want someone from his rank, which is definitely not I." Over the past two years I had been excluded from settlement socials, mostly from my own fault.

"Ah, but those wolf-like eyes spoke admiration." She refilled our goblets, emptying the flask.

I was not the only one to notice his eyes.

"Granddaughter, enjoy his regard!" She wagged her finger in mock scolding. "You should have at least three children by now."

"How?" I playfully grasped her hand.

"Well," she chuckled, "several warriors in the village are interested in you."

"Who?"

She shook her head with a naughty wink. "I'm not telling. Their lust would be more of a bother than an enjoyment."

"Grandmother!" I feigned shock with a giggle. In her culture these thoughts were acceptable amusement. Within mine, they were vulgar and shameful.

"Go to bed, girl."

She slapped my thigh and returned to the chapel.

Chapter 4

Lying in bed, warmed by Nanny lying next to me, my thoughts returned to what Soujeesh had said.

"That man is worthy of you."

She'd never said this of Andrew Nettles. She had said nothing; neither had Papa. I might have married Andrew had he agreed to free the six men who worked his land.

He had refused. "Your precious Joseph Brant was a slave owner, so don't get indignant with me."

"I can't change that," I had defended, "but I can do something about The Forty."

He accepted my work with African fugitives at the mission, but forbid me from interfering with his workers at The Forty. They were well treated and would be freed when legally required. He expected to be financially compensated by the Crown, in return.

"And will you pass that compensation on to them for their stolen lives?" I had persisted.

He never answered me.

Soon after, he had taken Anne Van Aston as his wife. Her placid nature suited him better.

Eventually we made peace. I avoided social awkwardness by no longer attending socials at The Forty. When Papa was brought home from York, it was Andrew who dug the grave. That was when he first brought up my working as governess. He even offered to give reference to the Canada West Mission Board, which he served on. I had argued to continue Papa's work at Elbema Falls. The church would send a replacement, he had insisted, for both teaching and ministry at The Forty. Unless I married a Reverend, I was no longer of use.

Though ordained by the Church of England, Papa's Quaker leanings encouraged me to believe opportunity was open to both man and woman. Praying "Thy Kingdom come, Thy will be done on Earth as it is in heaven," he interpreted as a call to roll up sleeves and get started bringing it about. That's what we did at the mission with our school and healing care, as well as with Papa's pastoral duties; and that's what I hoped to further after the war.

More than food and good wine were needed to stir my heart again. Until today, I had not met a wit that matched mine, except for Papa. The Captain was different. When I had my say, he listened and met me with consideration, not condescension. His written commendation of Sammy's service was unexpected thoughtfulness. He obviously knew I was hiding the lad from conscription and had shown understanding at the lad's plight.

*****

The *Dominion* sailed during the night. I awoke to the delicious aroma of brewing coffee, pulled on my trousers and thick wool sweater, and hurried down to the kitchen. Two chickens squawked at me from their cages by the door.

"Soon we might have eggs." Martha poured me a mug of coffee and handed me a scone. "Not today, though. Those birds need to settle down and get comfortable before they can lay."

I finished off a second scone before going out to the chapel. Simon and Mathew had made it through the night and now rested in quiet stupor. This would be a good time to work away at the unfinished graves. I returned to the kitchen just long enough to ask Martha to bring out a bucket of coals, then went in search of the shovel.

The left barn door hung ajar, the latch damaged—likely through the haste of those sailors. I balanced it for later repair and opened the other side. If the thaw continued, the chickens might be soon moved out here.

I was greeted by a brisk rustle among the hay as I entered the barn—probably just a squirrel. The shovel was not in its usual place next to the door. The sailors had left it leaning against the rear door. I crossed the barn floor and reached for it, but a sharp click to the side caught my attention.

A musket raised. I faced a boy clothed in shabby deerskin, crouching in the rear stall. He seemed just as startled as I.

After Andrew's warning of a renegade American, I had not expected someone so young. From his grubby appearance he had obviously had a rough go for some time. I would have thought him harmless, but he was terrified and kept the musket to my face. His eyes fixed on me as he backed deeper into the stall.

"Did you get separated from your people?" I asked.

He shivered, his face clouding with dread. Soujeesh had walked quietly in and now stood beside me.

"What's that idiot want?" she barked.

His musket traced the space between us and he blinked in panic.

"You have only one shot, so who's it going to be?" Soujeesh grumbled impatiently. "If you shoot her, I'll slit your throat."

"And if you harm my grandmother, I'll slit your gut." I followed in her stream. "So how do you want to die, fast or slow?"

His eyes opened wider. Our attempt to manage only worsened the situation. Fortunately, Martha marched in just then with the bucket of hot coals.

"Did y'all find that shovel?" Astutely, she took in the standoff and calmly asked, "When did you last eat, son?"

His eyes darted frantically between the three of us.

"Point that gun elsewhere, before you hurt someone," she persisted, unflustered. "This is a Christian mission."

"The—they—ain't talking Christian," he blurted out.

"And I don't blame them. They been working half the night trying to keep alive men wounded by you

Americans. So they're short on nice." Martha paused to let him digest her words. "Now follow me into the kitchen and I'll fix you something to eat. I'll see you're safely on your way after you pay us back by helping finish those graves. You have my word on that."

"We have work to do," Soujeesh declared, and left.

I followed her to the chapel leaving Martha to manage the boy.

Simon and Mathew lay near the brazier fire. Nanny sat between, reading from the book of Psalms. Simon was awake and welcomed a mug of whiskey. Mathew shivered with fever, barely conscious. I could only manage a few drops of castoreum under his tongue with a sip of water, and did my best adjusting the binding of his remaining leg. Balancing it tightly enough to support the leg without stopping blood flow made the difference between knitting the bone properly and gangrene.

By the time I returned from the chapel, the graves were deep enough for burial. I asked the boy to help bring out the bodies. He refused.

"I don't bury British." He set the shovel against the fence, next to his musket and folded his arms. His shoulders slumped with fatigue.

"See those crosses?" I pointed out the front row of the cemetery. "They're likely Americans washed up on the shore, since no one has come to claim them. I did them proper 'cause we're all made in the image of God."

He groaned and followed me back into the chapel. We carried the two out to the cemetery. Nanny and Martha joined us at the graves and I read the Service of Burial.

After singing a few hymns, we lowered them into the grave. The boy stood off to the side watching in sober silence, while we took turns with the shovel.

"I need to find my people." He took up his musket from the fence.

"I can't help you there," I answered honestly, but gave him direction to those paths that skirted Mohawk camps and Niagara settlements. Martha made him up a sack of food.

"British food," I reminded him, before he disappeared up the escarpment path.

Andrew had been right after all. The American was known at the mission, but compassion is not treason.

Soujeesh returned to her village that afternoon. I would battle the fever and putrefaction over the next few weeks. Poultices, herbs, molds and maggots were my tools, not a surgeon's saw.

After settling the sailors that evening, I waited with Martha for her son's return. I threaded her needle for darning one of her Sammy's socks. Nanny had gone to bed early, fatigued from the events of the past two days.

"You're fearless," I offered in appreciation of her calm handling of the frightened American boy.

Her lips curled up in mute reply. Several minutes passed. She stretched the threadbare heel around the darning egg, her needle weaving in and out. My comment must have offended her. In the few months bode with us she had revealed little of her past.

"Oh, honey," she chuckled, quietly looking up from her work. "I am filled with fear. But if I gave it mind, I'd still be yoked in the Shenandoah."

She resumed working in poignant silence. I sensed she had more to say.

"How?"

She sighed with a gentle nod. "Sammy was going to be taken from me. I pleaded with the Lord to not let it be. And I had to trust Him—not my fear—and leap into troubled waters."

I knew the Bible story that she referenced about the healing pool of Bethesda. It told of a pond that, when the waters were stirred by angels, would bring new life to the first person who leapt in.

"How did you know those 'troubled waters' weren't worse?"

"I didn't." She shrugged. "Only looking back do I see the path we traveled. There was a monstrous storm. In the confusion we fled into the Appalachians, met kindly Cherokee and traveled north with them to Niagara. Now here we are."

"What will you do come spring?"

"We'll stay to see your crops in and then join other refugees up in York." She studied the sock in her hand. "I hear experienced housekeepers are hard to come by in that town. Seems they get high ideas, marry, and set up their own households." With a sharp stab of her needle she resumed her work. "I've a mind to do just that, as well."

I laughed. Until then I'd thought Martha old, but she wasn't. The Captain's commendation gave assurance Sammy would not be conscripted. Her vitality ensured they'd enjoy a full life.

Chapter 5

Sunny days lengthened and buds erupted out of barren branches. Sprouts reached up from the thawing earth and maple sap began to flow. A busy couple of weeks followed. Much of my time was taken up with Mathew and Simon. Dressings had to be frequently changed, wounds peeled, poultices applied and herbal elixirs consumed to hold infection at bay. Fortunately, Sammy took over collecting the maple sap, boiling it down to thick syrup.

The chickens, comfortably housed where the American had hidden, were beginning to lay eggs. I had taken a break from the chapel, in search of a few, when I heard a sonorous "MOO" out in the yard. A sailor waited outside, holding a cow by a leash.

From the beast's small stature, thick coat and stocky limbs I knew she was of the sought-after *Canadienne* breed. French Canadian farmers had brought these hearty cattle from France over 200 years ago and improved upon the breed to withstand harsh Canadian winters.

"Gooday, miss. She's a fine one!" He touched his forelock in respect.

I walked over, kissed the cow's pale fawn muzzle, caressed its well-muscled limbs and firm udder, and declared my agreement.

He watched me, feet shifting awkwardly. My trousers made him uncomfortable. Shipboard gossip was certain to follow and there was not much I could do about it. To ignore his uneasiness was the best course. I had done nothing wrong; his thoughts were the problem.

I directed him to the remaining empty stall and asked him to settle her there. The Captain waited in the vicarage, he replied, keeping his eyes fixed on his feet.

Nanny was with the Captain, by the hearth. From her scowl I knew I must change before joining them. The Captain just smiled.

I hurried up to my room and put on my reliable brown dress and green shawl. Nanny had gone to fetch her knitting basket when I returned.

"Thank you for the cow, sir. She's a fine one," I offered in greeting.

"You were right!" he returned. "A good amount of influence was needed to get that cow."

"You've been most considerate with Sammy Smith's commendation," I added. "And we've been eating quite well—along with your men, of course, and..." my thoughts flitted to that nameless American boy, "others in need."

"Then repay me with a cup of your herbal concoction. I must say, that brew did pick me up."

I prepared him a pot and invited him to the table.

"Have you a surgeon aboard your ship?" I felt protective of his men. They were in no shape to leave. Skin had not yet thickened over their stumps and they risked infection.

"I set him ashore in Kingston long ago. He was a drunkard and a butcher and did more harm than good."

"You released him to hurt others?"

"No Miss Blythe. He only hurts himself, roaming about in a drunken stupor. It is a rare surgeon who can keep both compassion and sanity."

Whether this was praise or insult, I did not know. I was always on the defensive about my work. Andrew Nettles protested Soujeesh's influence in my life and insisted that, should we marry, my nursing be limited to our family, for decency sake.

Nanny returned and joined us for tea. When finished, we went out to the chapel. Both Mathew and Simon were awake, talking with Martha. The Captain greeted them enthusiastically, encouraging them to give full attention to preparing for their new life after the war. His words left them with hope—life's greatest tonic.

Out in the bright sunlight, he turned to me. "You and Soujeesh have done much good in giving life back to those two."

"Have we? They have been revived to suffer." I paused. "Is that goodness?"

I craved assurance at that moment. We were over the worse with Mathew and Simon, but they now faced a painful struggle adjusting to maimed bodies.

"Janet." He took my hand and my heart warmed—only Nanny called me Janet. "They suffer because of war. Of that I am equally guilty." His thumb slowly moved over my fingers in a gentle caress. "Your skills must be used for good, that is your duty. Leave the consequence to providence and have mercy on yourself. We all fail, the Good Lord knows that."

Both touch and words brought comfort. He let go of my hand with a squeeze and asked if Nanny was my grandmother.

"She was my mother's nanny and companion," I answered.

"Why did your father choose to minister here? I have heard he was an educated man."

The question surprised me. What had education to do with a choice of conscience?

"If I am to share family secrets, so must you," I answered.

"Quite right! Let's enjoy this fine day."

I looked in on Nanny to tell her we were off for a walk. She asked I wait and went out to have a quick word with the Captain. I assumed it was regarding the care of his men. Almost immediately she was back and planted a light kiss on my cheek.

"Mind that young man, lass." Her face crinkled in a smile. "He's nae familiar with our ways."

A walk was just what I needed. Though the weather had warmed, spring was still young and mosquitoes scarce. I lifted my skirt to avoid a puddle and felt his steadying hand on my arm. Previously I might have been offended by such a gesture. I was more than capable of navigating the muddy yard. Today, basking in the sunshine and gentle breezes off the lake, I took delight in the Captain's attentiveness.

"I'm a second son and share the plight of many a British officer in Canada," he began. "As you know, under the law, it is the older brother who inherits all, so I must make my way in the world. After grammar school, I entered His Majesty's Navy to do just that." He glanced back at the sailor watching from the barn door. "How did your family come to the wilds of Canada?"

I hardly heard his question, thinking about a childhood so different from mine, with property, travel and opportunity. We continued along the path towards the base of the escarpment.

"You were to tell me of your family," he prompted.

"Papa was the ward of a wealthy family," I began. "His education was paid by a sponsor. Since he loved both science and faith, he chose the Church for it gave him freedom to pursue both. Coming to Canada gave him opportunity to live out his beliefs."

"I've noticed his small library is quite diverse." He hesitated, as if considering his words. "His death was a tragic loss to the settlement of Canada West."

"It should never have happened." I shuttered remembering his shrouded body carried ashore. "The Americans in York were hooligans. After they blew up the garrison magazine, all hell broke out, with looting and burning and…" I picked up the pebble at my feet and hurled it into the woods. "They shot him in the back, you know—he wasn't even armed."

"No words can comfort such cruel injustice." He returned my hand within his arm and we continued towards the escarpment. As we walked, he mentioned seeing my mother's marker in the cemetery during the burial of Tom Haddon.

"She died giving birth to my brother, when I was just a babe. Neither survived. I believe she was of nobility."

"Believe?" he repeated before inquiring her family name.

"I don't know for sure."

"Shouldn't that interest you? You're a lively maid."

His comment pricked me because it had interested me, but both Nanny and Papa were always unsettled by my probing questions. They preferred to recount fond memories of early adventures in Canada. Nanny did provide a few vague vignettes of my mother's youth describing her prosperous family in Hertfordshire and her playful impulsive nature. Nothing was said of her family connections, however, or how she came to London as a young woman. Papa was an orphan so provided little of his family except that they were tenant farmers. He met my mother at a London charity where they both ministered. I did not push for more.

"I doubt there is scandal," I advanced with conviction. "If it was important, Papa would have told me."

The captain winced. "We all have our secrets—even a vicar and his lady." He patted my hand. "Will you return to England, when your father's replacement comes, after the war?"

"I have no one in England. If I was a man I would apply for a land grant." I chuckled at my self-effacement.

"Change that! If I was a man I would get ordained and be my father's replacement!"

He smiled sagely. "First let's bring an end to this war, aye?"

We had arrived at the heavily wooded base of the escarpment. This was the path up the rocky cliffs by which Sammy traveled to Soujeesh and the American boy had fled. The sound of splashing water traveled through the trees. Snowmelt flow lasted only a few weeks, but was enough to add "Falls" to Elbema's name. The rest of the year the flow was a mere trickle, except during storms.

"Your connection with Andrew Nettles seems far more personal than neighbors," he ventured.

I let go of him, taken back by his forwardness.

"Pray, forgive me," he immediately offered.

I accepted his apology, assuming shipboard life and the war had eroded his manners.

"If you must know, Andrew Nettles and I were friends in youth, and we did talk of a possible understanding. He is much better suited with the lass he settled on. Marriage should be a match of wit and vision."

"I heartily agree." He held out his arm and I again slipped mine within. "And you remain without a suitor?"

"I have yet to find my match," I provided honestly. "With this war, I've little time for courtship. And if you have heard good spoken of my father, you probably know that he raised me with ideals that can deter—"

"Extraordinary!" he cut in. "He raised you to be extraordinary, is what I've heard. And you must always stay true to that."

I savored every step of our slow return to the mission. His admission to making inquiries of me brought lightness to my step. We spoke of nothing of consequence; I enjoyed my arm entwined with his.

"Do you ride?" he asked, upon return to the vicarage.

"Yes, but only astride," I replied.

He brought my fingers to his lips with a soft kiss before letting go.

From the landing, I watched until his longboat disembarked onto the HMS *Dominion*. Perhaps I had acted with undue familiarity. It had been a long time since I had enjoyed pleasant engagement and I hoped for more with him in the future. Perhaps I had found my match.

Chapter 6

Mid-June 1814

Days stretched into weeks until a month passed without the Captain's return. Sugaring off was over and the kitchen garden planted. The sailors in the chapel were on the mend, managing with little infection. Simon moved about, adapting to the use of his other arm.

Mathew was not so fortunate. His remaining leg could not yet bear weight and the stump of the other remained tender. At Nanny's request Andrew Nettles brought up a few pieces of pine, I found sketches of Papa's ideas for a peg and Mathew was tasked to make it, with Simon's help.

Seeing Andrew again was good. I had dressed in my flowery muslin dress and the summer sun put me in a good mood. We talked of crops and weather and then he proudly announced that Anne was again with child. I wished him well, relieved that this was not my lot. It is not that I don't want children—perhaps someday—but since Papa's death a vague dissatisfaction had stirred within me, as if something waited for me.

The conversation soon bored me—or perhaps it was only Andrew. It seemed as if he was trying to stir up envy. I had my fill and announced that we had too many eggs before escaping to the barn to fetch him some. The sacrifice of those eggs was worth his amicable send-off.

Mathew and Simon worked quite well together. One had legs, the other had arms, and making a peg leg gave them something useful to do, to rebuild strength. When they were strong enough, we intended to have them help in the fields to further their usefulness. Sammy and Martha had delayed leaving to help me put in a mixed field of corn, squash and beans. Soon they would depart.

The heat of the day was not yet upon us when Sammy ran up from the shore. He had a hungry look about him. I had been churning butter for over an hour and had worked up a sweat. That last part of churning was the most difficult, as the cream began to thicken into butter.

"There's a ship anchored out near The Forty." He flashed his best smile. "Are those biscuits ready?"

"This churning is almost done so I can't really stop, but…" I shrugged. Maybe he was hungry enough to finish up those last tough strokes in exchange for a sack of biscuits and dried apple pieces. "If you churn, I'll fetch you a feast."

"Naw, that women's work," he bargained, aware of my reasoning.

"So is baking biscuits. What do you want?"

With a conceding shrug he took the paddle. I lingered in the kitchen, chatting with Martha, to ensure his strong arms finished the job.

When I returned, I found Captain Cliveton dismounted in the barnyard. He led a second horse behind his own and had tied them both to a cemetery fence post.

"Ahoy, Miss Blythe." He greeted me pleasantly, as if only a day had passed, not a month. "I've come to see how Simon and Mathew are faring."

I passed the sac of food to Sammy and took the paddle. After such a passage of time, it was obvious the Captain had not come for me.

"You could have spared the horse, sir. They're far from ready to leave, let alone ride."

"I was actually hoping that we might ride after I look in on my men."

While he was in the chapel, I carried the churn into the kitchen. I intended to refuse his offer and declared so to Martha. His presumption that I might still be interested was vexing, after all this time.

"Don't you be a silly girl," she scolded gently. "I can set these in the molds. A nice ride will do you good—more than nursing your bruised pride."

I joined Captain Cliveton in the chapel. Again he praised the progress of his men's healing. Praise for my work? A ride in appeasement? This was not enough after the confidences of the last visit. I had felt his absence and wanted him to feel the same.

Today I would ensure he would remember me.

I invited him to barn and asked him to wait while I climbed the ladder to the loft; Papa's clothes were stored up there in a trunk.

"Whatever are you rummaging for?" the Captain asked.

"Your riding clothes." I tossed them down along with a pair of moccasins. Then, I slipped off the brown wool dress I wore because of Simon and Mathew being about. Underneath I still wore work trousers and a linen shirt, should I need to go to the squash field.

He shook out the buckskin outfit and looked up with a frown. "I can't wear moccasins. I need solid footing."

"Too Canadian for you, Captain?" I climbed down. "Where I want to ride you can't let European vanity get in the way."

He looked me up and down, tilted his head and smirked. "I'm not vain Janet," he said softly, "and my name is James."

I waited behind the barn with the horses while he changed. When he came out, I liked what I saw. He moved more freely in these clothes than the Navy issue. My disposition also improved with his acceptance of my lead.

With a stab of my foot in the stirrup, I leapt onto the mare's back. A saddle was luxury, to my usual bareback ride.

"I must be back to The Forty by early evening." He nudged his mount forward with a soft tap of the foot. "Until then, lead me astray!"

"We're up the mountain, James," I proclaimed, with a heel to the flank of my mare.

Off I led. At the foot of the escarpment I steered my horse onto the rugged path. Upward we continued, faster and faster, until we were almost racing. Near the top, the trail narrowed and steepened. I hugged tight to my steed, holding her to the center in an effort to block him. He inched forward, nudging my horse against the mountain. With a loud "whoop" he squeezed by and leapt ahead.

"Brilliant!" I yelled at his back.

The path was steepest just before the top. He eased his pace, forcing me to hold my horse to a walk. I suspect he wanted to savor the breeze moving through the leafy canopy above. Dappled sunlight danced through gaps in the branches. Light scattered about us like playful fairies. Cautiously we guided our horses over the rocky ledge, into the small clearing. Emerging from the forest's protection, we met a gusty wind off the great lake.

"Where do we go from…" He turned and fell silent. The view captured him as I hoped it would.

This was my favorite place, looking out towards the eastern horizon. Time appeared to seamlessly join with space. The Great Ontario Lake stretched before us, waters meeting sky in an uninterrupted flow of past into present. There were no limits here, nothing to come between my dreams and my world.

Two hawks glided above in a wide smooth circle. Unencumbered, oblivious to us, they hunted to the symphony of wind-tussled foliage. James looked up and his face lit with childlike joy.

"They shall mount up with wings as eagles," he whispered.

One of those graceful creatures dropped in a sudden dive to the valley below.

"Beautiful, aren't they?" I offered, hoping to enter his thoughts. "Fortunate to be unfettered."

"I used to hunt with a falcon when I was a boy." He looked at me intently. "To be free, as they are now, would be wonderful."

The remaining hawk rose higher towards the noon-day sun, circling in an ever-widening search for prey.

"Europeans rarely enjoy this vantage. They prefer the familiar shore."

"This is how we should see it, Janet." His eyes crinkled pleasantly. "This is a glimpse of eternity."

"York is over there." I pointed to the faint grey plume on the horizon. To the south I could see his ship anchored. "There's your *Dominion*, James."

"Aye. I'm berthed off The Forty."

"There's my ship," I said, pointing across to an old tree.

"Your ship?" he laughed.

Unbeknownst to Nanny, when younger I would rush through my chores to pass many a day in the tree's branches. The richness of my mind transformed my oak into a sea-faring vessel. I even spoke of her just as sailors in Burlington Heights talked of their ships. Now jutting over the ridge at a dangerous angle, the next ice storm would send her plummeting into the canyon depth below.

"Aye. I sailed the seven seas of my imagination in that tree."

"As a young man, I did sail the seven seas."

His comment silenced me. I had lived a vivid life in my mind, but had seen so little of the world. My horse stomped and tossed her head impatiently. She was ready to run again. So was I.

"Where to now?" He squinted at the sun.

"Soujeesh's village."

I steered my horse onto the narrow trail into the woods. He followed in silence. Light trickled about us through the quivering leaves. We rode for about a mile, feeling no need to speak. A few times I glanced back and met his boyish look of delight. The path opened out into a grassy meadow where Mohawk warriors trained their few cherished horses. Smoke from the village was visible in the distance.

"Catch me if you can!" I teased, with a nudge to my horse's flank. She answered with a lively jump, and off we flew.

Anticipating my move, he surged ahead without warning. Following hard, I ducked the clods of dirt flung back by his horse. Hunkering against mine, I managed to catch up. By midfield we were racing side by side. We had almost crossed the meadow when I remembered the gorge before the village, where the streambed cut. Though shallow, it might endanger the horses.

"Ditch ahead!" I screamed and pulled hard on my reins.

Both horses reared in response. We were both sweaty and giddy when we eased our horses into a cooling trot and continued toward the gully. Down the shaded bank we followed the course, towards the village. Neither of us conceded defeat, nor did we claim victory. Our giddiness erupted into nervous laughter, realizing how close we'd come to disaster.

At the widest span of the creek he dismounted and reached up for me. Without hesitation I found myself in his arms. He spun me around with a playful embrace before setting me on my feet. Standing in his arms, I made no move, but looked up to meet his gaze. Drawing me ever closer, he tenderly stroked my cheek, fingers straying to the nape of my neck. He lingered, waiting for a response. Warmth flowed over me at his tentative advance. I closed my eyes and his lips brushed gently over mine. Pulling me closer, his kisses matched my hunger. All awareness ceased, except for an intoxication of longing. Then, abruptly, he pulled away.

His face was flushed and his gaze fixed on me, almost pleading. I was confused. What had I done to displease him?

Without a word, he took the reins of both horses and walked away, towards the village.

Hurrying behind I tried to ask what had happened, but a hoard of boisterous village children jumped into the gully, intercepting me.

"Janie! Janie! You have a man!" they squealed excitedly in Mohawk. "And he's an Englisher!" A few shrewd ones demanded to know if I had brought them any maple treats, before propelling me to the village shouting, "We must show Soujeesh!"

James tethered the horses and caught up as we entered the village. I glanced at him unable to decipher his face. He looked intently ahead.

Women poured out from bark-covered longhouses, drawn by the commotion of the children. Surrounded by clamorous greetings, we continued on to the main lodge where Soujeesh waited in the doorway.

"Granddaughter!" She greeted in Mohawk. "I was hoping to see you once more. I have just been summoned to Moravian Town. That west is still disputed!" With a nod at James, she continued in English, "You are looking quite well, Captain Cliveton. Deerskin becomes you."

"Tolerance, you mean." He bowed to her with good-humored flourish and kissed her hand.

"Come and share food," she cackled, leading us into the longhouse.

He acted as if nothing were amiss. His hand glanced across my back, while his eyes remained ahead as we entered. I was frustrated at my inability to interpret his thinking.

Around a central smoky fire we sat, eyes slowly adjusting to the dim light. The communal shelter was pleasantly cool and smoldering aromatic leaves kept mosquitoes away. The women joined us and the few older men who sat to one side. The warriors must already have gone west to Moravian Town.

Mugs of tea and chunks of freshly baked cornbread were passed around as James thanked Soujeesh for the work she had done on Simon and Mathew. She nodded quietly and lit a ceremonial pipe. After a long draw she passed it to him. He partook and passed it to me. I drew deep and allowed the pipe to continue around the fire. Those present began to exchange news. James was politely attentive, though primarily Mohawk was spoken. When conversation abated, he stood and began an eloquent description of his hope for peaceful settlement of the many peoples within Canada.

Masterfully he commandeered the attention of all present with impressive gestures and poignant pauses. He spoke in English with exaggerated gestures that left no doubt of how important he believed his message.

While his spirit was impressive, his bias for British colonization and Native dependency was naively ignorant. Soujeesh folded her arms with a hardened face, waiting for him to finish. The rest sat in silence, not understanding sufficient English to be offended. With a bow, he finished undeterred and thanked Soujeesh for her hospitality.

"Pray, excuse me," he then said. "I must hasten back, for I am expected tonight at The Forty."

Soujeesh accompanied us to the horses. "Go in peace my children," she said and then added in Mohawk, "and go wisely, grand-daughter."

We quickly retraced our path through the meadow. My heart was heavy. His was the first passionate embrace I had ever returned and I naively presumed he felt the same. Instead he seemed to retreat from me and use our time to plead the British cause before a representative of the Mohawk Council.

At the edge of the escarpment we paused for one final look over the lake. The sun was at our backs and soon would set.

He reached for my hand and gently pressed his lips to my palm. "Thank you for this enjoyable day, Janet."

What had he enjoyed with me? The hawks? The kiss? My pipe smoking? Or the access he had, through Soujeesh, to reach the Council?

I pulled away and led us down the mountain. His *soirée* was only a few miles south along the Mohawk road, at the Forty. I would have wanted to go with him, but was not invited. Andrew Nettles would be there, of course. I only hoped that I would be spoken well of that evening.

At the barn, James quickly changed into his uniform, leaving my father's clothes neatly folded atop the trunk.

"Godspeed," he said and rode off with the horses.

Chapter 7

Two months passed; two bloody months.

The Americans attacked Canada with renewed vengeance. Blood had soaked Lundy's Lane, further south, in the raging fight to drive the Americans back. The American capital of Washington was burned to the ground. In Lower Canada, the British army retreated north from Lake Champlain, to Montreal. On the Western frontier, the Americans were forced across the Niagara peninsula and besieged in a final stronghold at Fort Erie. Both sides committed atrocities. In the final draw neither side ceded defeat. Canada had survived, unabsorbed by the Americans. The Americans had evaded re-absorption by Britain.

Soujeesh did not return to the Niagara village, but remained in the west. Settlers returned back to their farms, Sammy and Martha had gone on to York, and I was left to reflect on the foolish liberty I had allowed James. I would see him at least once more when he returned for his men.

Up on the escarpment my faithful oak tree was dying. Yellow leaves checkered sparse foliage. Many branches were now barren and the cracked bark easily broke away. I climbed within the branches one last time, mindful that her roots might soon give way and release their tentative hold on the earth. Gazing out through the branches, I remembered the dreams of my youth, thanked her for those voyages and looked over the lake, hoping for sight of the *Dominion.*

Soujeesh had warned me to go wisely. It was too late. Though the time together had been brief, our lively exchanges drew me to him. His caresses up on the escarpment only drove deeper his invasion of my heart.

I prayed for his safe return and then I prayed for clear thinking. Like the words of Papa's song, I no longer knew if I sank or swam.

In late August, on a hot summer day, he strode into our yard. I was under the shade of the apple tree, shucking peas. I stood in greeting, tipping over my basket in the process. He bowed, set my basket aright and knelt to scoop up the scattered pods. The weary officer had returned poised and victorious. His careful grooming and smart uniform contrasted with my shabby dress.

"It is a far different world than when last I visited," he ventured.

I looked out over the thickly matted field, where Simon and Mathew were doing their best to cut stalks. We'd planted the "three sisters" of corn, squash and beans there, following the Mohawk practice. The men's work was made difficult as they frequently tripped over the squash and clinging bean vines. Nanny insisted physical work was appropriate repayment. They attempted to meet her expectation.

"I find you looking well," I said, finally looking back at him.

"Miss Blythe, I've come for my men," he hesitated, his voice hoarse.

"There they are, sir," I said, pointing to the field, "mended and put to good use. Such work both helps them adjust and restores dignity. What can't be cured must be endured, eh?"

"Will you also press me into service to mend me?" he asked.

Our eyes met. I wasn't going to bite the bait. He had returned a stranger.

"Shall we have tea?" I invited him inside to the cool parlor we had made in Papa's former study. He sat on the settee. "Forgive my appearance, Captain," I said awkwardly. "I've little time to preen."

"You are most becoming, Janet, in anything you wear." His gentle jest rekindled what I had fought to suppress these past two months. "And has that cow fulfilled the value I put on her?"

"Yes," I said softly, and an unsettling pause ensued.

"I cannot comprehend why hot tea on a hot afternoon is so refreshing." His hand glanced mine as he took the cup. I recoiled as if I had been stung.

"One of the mysteries of life." I was at a loss for something clever to say. "It is a much richer cup I serve you than the last one—it's real tea," I ventured.

"There could never be a more heartening cup," he protested pleasantly. "Peace is near, Janet, and I had hoped to be stationed, perhaps nearby at Fort George. If I had more opportunity—"

The room filled with promise at what he was about to say, but it was cut short by Nanny's brusque entrance. He stood as she crossed the floor to sit with us.

"It is good to see you are in good health, Captain Cliveton." She snatched up her sewing basket. "Will you linger to enjoy a meal with us? We have enough for you and your oarsmen."

"I cannot impose any further," he replied.

"But, y-you must stay for a meal of fine venison," I urged. "Please—before you take your men away. I shot the deer myself with my new musket!"

"Both healer and huntress are you?" He shook his head with amusement. "You may not be rid of all of us. Some are staying on in Canada as they are eligible for a pension."

"Will you be as fortunate?" I dared ask.

"I am not free from duty," he hesitated. "What will you do when your father's replacement comes?"

I looked down, but said nothing and the room fell silent. His question felt like a slap. Elbema Falls was the only home I had ever known. Andrew had requested a minister for the mission. I still clung to the hope that I might run the school.

We ate a harvest meal outside in the grove. Steaming potatoes, roasted vegetables and venison were set out in a feast I could have only dreamt of last winter. Chairs were brought out and a makeshift table was made of wood planks covered with white linen sheets. Mathew, Simon and the oarsmen ate seated on the ground around us.

"I shall dearly miss…" He failed again to complete whatever he intended to say.

"Before the war, my time was filled with Papa's work," I prompted. "With peace again here, I want to re-open the mission school. If not here, perhaps further west in a new settlement."

He smiled warmly. "I would expect nothing less of you. Not many would own such diligence, but won't you find it confining to live among savages?"

His bias could not be ignored. "Who are those savages, sir? Those displaced Native people up on the escarpment or the ones who drove them there?"

His eyes hardened. He said nothing, provoking me further.

"You British still don't respect our sacrifices in this war. Land and compensation is allocated by preference to those of British stock. Loyal Natives and Africans don't get their due. And what about women? Will Mrs. Secord ever be—"

"I refuse to debate the Crown's position," he cut me off.

"And I refuse to stay silent to injustice!" I snapped back.

"And *I* insist you let the man have his pie and be on his way!" Nanny dropped a heaping plate between us.

We were not finished, only interrupted.

"Janet," he said my name with surprising gentleness. "My time here is short and I want to enjoy your company. Pray, do not hold me responsible for Britain's lapse of justice. I am just a sailor."

"Are you not in possession of your attitude?" I grew subdued. "And when you wear the King's uniform, do you not also represent him?"

"You mean well," he said, stabbing his fork into the pie. "Pray, treat me with same mercy you reserve for the downtrodden."

"Then you do concede justice is for all loyal Canadians?" I desired agreement in these remaining moments.

"Dear woman, forgive my uniform and the world I cannot change. And promise..." He grasped my hand firmly as if he would never let go. My candor had not come between us. "Promise me, Miss Blythe, to remain true to your heart. You hold convictions not many would have the courage to express, let alone follow." He let me go. "Though our opinions may differ, you will always have my highest regard."

Abruptly he stood. "I am summoned to York. Pray, understand my sincere desire has always been to return here. Your household is a great comfort in these times."

Nanny and I bid a sad goodbye to Simon and Mathew at the landing and watched until James Cliveton's longboat reached the *Dominion*.

"Your Papa gave you book learning, lass," she said, turning to me with a sigh, "but he did little to prepare you for the ways of gentlemen."

Whatever Nanny meant didn't matter. He had urged my heart to remain true. That must mean he would return, for he had said that was his desire.

Chapter 8

Papa's replacement arrived in early September. Andrew Nettles brought Reverend Cameron, his wife, their five children and their two servants down from Burlington Heights. After we were introduced Andrew explained that, with changes from the war, the mission's focus would now shift from being an outreach to the Mohawk refugees to pastoring settlers at The Forty. A larger church and proper rectory were to be built closer to the village, the mission would close and the clergy lands would be offered for lease. The reverend apologized on behalf of the mission board for not warning us in advance of the change of direction.

"We must not hinder progress!" he declared with a stubborn jut of his jaw.

Mrs. Cameron made no effort to hide her discouragement with the Niagara posting. Their previous parsonage had been in a large town in Sussex. After the difficult passage over the Atlantic and inland canoe trip she had been led to believe she was coming to a village rectory.

"It soon will be," her husband soothed.

We agreed to stay out the week at Elbema Falls and help his wife adjust to her new role as farmwife. I showed the reverend about the buildings, entrusting him with the cemetery catalogue of possessions saved from those dead washed ashore.

"Should kin come searching after the war, this may bring closure," I explained.

He sputtered awkwardly at our undertaking of such gruesome duty.

As we returned to the house, he indicated that he had come with an offer for me of a position as governess to three daughters of a retired British officer in Kingston. A place for Nanny was also included, as a housemaid, as well as a letter of credit to cover our passage.

Clearly I had cultivated herbs, not influential friends. Soujeesh's training did not open any means of support, neither did my education under Papa, except as a governess. I had no choice but to accept this humbling proposal of servitude.

"Fret not, Miss Blythe," the reverend cajoled. "You'll soon find yourself an officer with a small pension. There are plenty to be had—the pick of the crop—for a fine Christian woman such as yourself!"

Our only escape from these humiliating circumstances seemed to be mercenary marriage.

Reverend Cameron had no interest in the mission's farming operations. Andrew Nettles promised workers to help with the farm until the proposed rectory was readied at The Forty. The Reverend naively assumed it imminent. He would soon find out that settlers took care of their own lands before tending to the needs of the Church. Like most European newcomers, he did not realize he was expected to labor alongside them.

It soon became apparent I had been asked to stay the week to do Mrs. Cameron's work, rather than tutor her. She preferred to gossip about The Forty and I could give her little. Nanny patiently tried to explain about maple sugaring, soap and candle making, and peculiarities of frontier life, such as the need for mosquito smudge pots to ward off ague. I harvested the garden and prepared the vegetables for winter storage.

Mrs. Cameron assumed the livestock at the mission were hers. I baulked at her presumption. The chickens I could easily let go, but my cow was a gift from James Cliveton.

"She's intended for the Native village up on the escarpment," I lied. The village had moved further west, closer to Lake Erie. I had little choice about the cow. She could not come to Kingston, so I resolved to get as much as I could for her.

"How much did they offer?" Mrs. Cameron countered sharply.

She halved my overstated figure, but I held to my price, throwing in our linens, dishes and furnishings. I had already given my musket to a Mohawk warrior. To burn and butcher my possessions would please me more than satisfying her with a bargain. With a huff of obvious resentment, she accepted my terms. I cared not what she thought of me. Besides, Andrew had likely warned her of my demanding tenacity.

I gathered my favorite books from Papa's library and those that might help me as governess, and packed up a few to send to Sammy in York. The rest I left for the Camerons to share within the congregation or for the future schoolmaster. Last of all, on the eve of our departure, I tidied my family's graves one last time. *Love alters not*. I caressed the worn lettering of my mother's cross, knowing my return to this part of Canada would not be soon.

*****

Amidst the turmoil of that last week at Elbema Falls, a lone soldier strode into the vicarage yard. Mrs. Cameron rushed out of the cottage brandishing her broom high and screeching loudly. Nanny ran out behind her.

"Have a care, dear woman!" He grasped her broom with wide-eyed amusement.

"Mrs. Cameron!" I shouted in effort to defuse the encounter. "We are a mission and this loyal soldier must be need of sustenance."

She returned inside, huffing loudly about my cavorting about with soldiers. The slam of the cabin door sent the chickens into brief flight.

"I need to hasten on to Burlington, Miss Blythe, but I was charged to deliver this." He touched his forelock in a gesture of respect. "My condolences to the loss of your father. It's too late to matter, but you should still have this."

He thrust a tattered and stained letter into my hand. It was addressed to my father and the red wax bore a prominent crest. I stuffed the note into my pocket unread and wished the soldier "Godspeed."

When I showed Nanny the letter that evening, she gasped. "It's the Eldenmont Seal!"

Delaying reading Papa's letter had kept him with me for that brief while. I imagined him in his study waiting for it.

Finally, I broke open the seal. Nanny hovered nearby, silently watching me read. I confirmed it was indeed from a Charles Eldenmont and that it gave Papa permission for me to stay at the Eldenmont estate of Hurstmere, in Hertfordshire, England. The vague wording left me unsure if this was an offer of employment or I was invited as a guest.

"You'll be more than a guest, for sure," Nanny hissed. "How he caught up with you after all these years, I'll never know!"

Had Papa's journey to York something to do with this? His murder prevented my learning any plans he had made on my behalf.

"Who is this Charles Eldenmont?" I asked.

"You'll not reply!" she insisted. "You've no need of any help from that man." She quickly knelt, reaching under our bed and pulled out her small shabby trunk.

My whole life I'd seen this battered casket, assuming it held her modest belongings. Doubtless, its look of worn insignificance is why it was overlooked during the occupation. She took the key from the chain about her neck. Her hand shook as she pressed it in mine. "It was best you have not known about this. There is nothing to lose when you don't know you have it."

Within the box, wrapped in faded purple velvet, I found a set of silver candelabras, a silver plate and a leather pouch holding several delicate gold chains and pins, a pearl pennant, a plain gold ring, and a few silver coins.

"These are your treasures, Janet—your mother's property." Her eyes filled with tears. "I promised Cathy I would guard them for you."

I exhaled more in relief than sentiment. For a moment, I had had a horrid thought this cache might have been stolen. My body tingled as I ran my fingers over this tangible connection to the woman who had given me life. Papa had no images of her; only his memories. I caressed her possessions, regretting that I had never pressed to learn more of this woman.

"Did Papa agree to this?" I finally asked.

"They have nothing to do with your Papa. She asked me to keep them safe so you'd never be in want." She rubbed her sleeve against her eye and firmly ordered, "Forget that Eldenmont letter."

I repacked and locked the casket and kept the key. After she'd fallen asleep, I again opened the trunk to look at the articles. They spoke of a time of refinement and wealth, far from the outpost at Elbema Falls. My mother had come from a world different from what I knew. Touching them, I pondered her hopes for both herself and for me. I hardly slept that night.

"Would it have pleased my mother for me to work as governess out of choice, not necessity?" I asked Nanny early next morning, while waiting for Andrew to take us to Burlington Heights. "I want to keep her treasures, Nanny."

"Do as you see best," she answered tersely.

Chapter 9

Andrew Nettles did not come for us. Instead he sent Amos and his wagon to take us to Burlington Heights. I suppose he was too much of a coward to witness my eviction. The sun was still low in the sky when we left. Leaves had taken on vibrant hues of orange and red in a beautiful display of death. I spoke little to Amos on the long drive. Enough had been said in the past, when I argued with him to head north and earn his freedom in a lumber camp.

The autumn day turned out mild and bright and we arrived at the port just before noon. I searched for one final thing to say to Amos to mend our departure and be fondly remembered. He beat me to it.

"Miss Jane, life is not as simple as it appears," he declared when setting the last of our boxes down outside the door of the shipping office. "When we learn that, we are wise." And with a touch of his forelock he was gone.

I hoped to quickly secure passage across Lake Ontario, to Kingston. With favorable winds the sailing would take less than two days. The Colonel had arranged credit. I chose instead to purchase our passage with the money from Mrs. Cameron. I wanted to be free to leave should this position not be suitable.

I wrote a note of our situation for James Cliveton and would post it before sailing. Within me lingered a hope that I might chance upon him here. I did not view this as forward, for he had admitted that I had been a comfort to him these past few months.

The streets and taverns were busy. Though Fort Erie, on the western Niagara, was back in the hands of the Americans, settlers were returning to their farms. Winter was coming and they needed to salvage what they could before snow came. Lake Eire remained under control of the American fleet; the British fleet had regained Lake Huron and maintained secure control of Lake Ontario. War seemed soon to end. Out on the bay, two ships were anchored. Soldiers and settlers milled about the waterfront, impatient to board. Neither ship was the HMS *Dominion*.

I asked around and learned that the larger ship was a merchant vessel of the North West Trading Company, scheduled to sail directly to Kingston later that day. The other was a military vessel, also sailing for Kingston, with a stopover in York of at least two days.

I crossed the muddy road, worked my way through the crowd in the trading post with Nanny in my wake, and I set my letter on the counter. The clerk picked it up and playfully twirled it between his fingers.

"Keep your little love note, missy," he smirked. With a deft flick of his wrist, he returned it back to me. "The Captain has fled."

"Pardon?" His rudeness startled me. I could only assume that he had not properly read the address of my note. "The letter is for Captain Cliveton of the HMS *Dominion*, stationed here in Canada," I explained.

"I sees a lot 'ere girl." With a cheeky wink he leaned towards me. "Your good cap'n's been decommissioned. He's already halfway 'cross the Atlantic. Talk is he's to wed a fine lady and finally be free of common offerings."

"Common?" With no possible misunderstanding on his part this time, I fired back. "Speak for yourself, you loathsome reeking toad!"

The bustling store went still at my outburst. Quiet mutters and twitters slowly filled the air. Those nearby moved closer to the counter hoping to catch more of our exchange.

A trading post is not just for business and trade; it also serves as a depot of indiscriminate news and gossip. Both are essential to bridge frontier isolation and nurture endurance. Free exchange at the trading post leaves it to the listener to glean. What is refuse to one can be gold to another.

Nanny gripped my arm and firmly propelled me back through the crowd and out the door. "Hush, girl! Keep your dignity!"

"Common," I seethed. "Nobody has ever called me that."

"Janet Blythe!" She hurried me across the muddy road to an empty bench. "Have you no sense?"

"It must be a lie," I protested. "Even Soujeesh favored him."

Yet, she had also warned me 'go wisely' I recalled.

"Soujeesh you say?" Nanny snorted. "I didn'a think any white man had her regard—save your Papa, of course." She squeezed my hand in an attempt at assurance. "Well, we can trust that idle talk will soon die if we give it no mind. After all, you and the Captain simply enjoyed harmless flirtation."

It was no flirtation! He had led me to believe more. *Forgive me that which I cannot change.* I groaned with recollection. My humiliating presumption had blinded me. He wasn't referring to naval duty but a fiancé in England.

Nanny rambled on as if to quell her own doubt. "Perhaps you've made much of the Captain's attention, Janet. In this time of war, we did our duty to the Crown and he availed himself of it."

He had availed himself of me. I had ignored consequences and foolishly thrown myself at him, only to be sampled and spurned. Naively I had assumed respect of my skills meant respect for me. But the care of war casualties usually fell to drunkards and whores. With my trousers, competitive spirit and even my pipe smoking, I had unwittingly fed that imagery. A cow and a horse ride he might kindly give, but he had deemed me beneath inclusion at a local *soirée*.

Nanny was wrong; talk would not soon die. Those stares and nods from strangers leaving the trading post already showed word of this stupid girl's quest for a captain was spreading. With my public outburst I had propelled myself deep into gossip's cesspool. Ripples were now spreading beyond my control. Perhaps I had been gossiped about for a while at The Forty. Perhaps that was why Andrew sent Amos instead of coming himself.

I looked down the road towards the beach and I recognized the crippled gait of a peg leg. It was Mathew Hendrick. Such a wondrous sign of Providence! He was just who I needed to speak with to clear up this misunderstanding. I shouted out to him as he approached.

He looked up with a smile of recognition.

"Miss Blythe! Mrs. Wallace! It is a wonder to see you here." He managed a slightly awkward bow on his peg and crutch.

"I'm off to take a governess position in Kingston," I volunteered. "Is the *Dominion* expected soon in harbor? I don't see it about."

"She'll be returning within the week." He looked out over the water.

A surge of relief filled me.

"Sadly, though," he continued, "Captain Lord Cliveton no longer sails her. He has left us for England."

I gasped.

"Aye." He frowned sadly, thinking we shared the same disappointment. "Praise be to God for serving under such a just man and for you dear ladies who kept me in the land of the living."

I felt as though I'd been stabbed. All strength left me and I caught only a few words of what he spoke to Nanny—

some mention of a holding north of Burlington Heights, where Mathew's married brother had registered the adjacent allotment. With a final salute, he bid us "Godspeed!"

Chapter 10

The abrupt shock of betrayal settled on me. I'd taken James at his word, naively trusting what he said. The foolish letter now burned in my hand. I tore it into a hundred pieces, scattering it onto the dung filled road.

"So much for that man's 'sincere desire,' eh Nanny?" I moaned. "He made a fool of me."

I marched back and forth in the muck, anger rousing my soul. "May I plague him, please God," I hissed. "May I haunt whatever happiness he hopes to have!" I looked back towards Elbema Falls and then to the lake. My stomach churned.

"Janet! Hush, girl!" She clutched my arm pulling me to the bench. "That man gave you attention, but...there was no harm done."

I wouldn't tell her how he'd stirred me to hope or that his touch consumed my thoughts. I might have abandoned myself to desire, had he not pushed me away.

"So 'tis Lord Cliveton?" She sighed and her shoulders slumped. "Well that certainly explains a lot. No mere captain has flirted with you, girl. He's a fancy, so you must banish him from your hopes. We're away to Kingston and another life."

What life? I was yoked just like Martha Smith. She had found a way. *I had to trust Him—not my fear—when He troubled the water.*

James Cliveton had provided Sammy Smith with a letter of commendation. I had received nothing. My mother's treasure might be enough to purchase property, but alone, as a woman, I was not eligible for a land allotment. Work as a governess insulted all my training with Soujeesh, and settling for an acceptable marriage bed felt like a step above prostitution. Niagara women did not dare tell of what they endured during the occupation for fear of losing reputation. What hope had I for my indiscrete behavior?

Gossip would taint me—if my uncommon upbringing hadn't already. No means of escape existed but out on the lake, in those anchored ships. That Eldenmont letter opened a door beyond Kingston and a new beginning. My mother's treasure made passage to England possible.

"We will accept that Eldenmont invitation," I pronounced.

"But the Colonel is expecting you," Nanny argued. "Shall we destroy your reputation?"

"I've naught to salvage, Nanny—today only worsens my lot. Every Niagara tavern will soon be twittering about this outburst. 'That misguided vicar's daughter—such a trollop—do you know what she's done now?' Do you think the Colonel will want me near his children when he hears how I threw myself after a British officer?"

"And what would your Papa say?" Nanny implored.

"He'd say that we've nowhere to go but up." I squared my shoulders and set off in the direction of the shipping office. "As a free woman, I can set my course."

She raced behind me, breathless. "Narrow-minded gossip will soon die—"

"But I will not die." My heart surged at this declaration. "Neither will I crawl under a rock and hide. If I must earn a living, it will not be in Canada."

"You know nothing of the Eldenmonts!" she protested, flushed with exertion.

"We'll arrive before any letter," I asserted. We had not a moment to lose, soon Montreal would freeze up and ship travel would shut down until spring. "I'd sooner be a governess over there, then here."

Our three trunks waited on the porch of the shipping office, where Amos had left them. I retrieved my letter from Charles Eldenmont and marched through the door, forcing through the crowd, up to the counter.

I rapped firmly on the desktop. "Arrange passage for me on the next ship bound for Kingston."

An oily man slowly looked up from his ledger with a half smile. "What's that you say, miss?" His smirk was just as horrid as that of the trading post clerk down the street.

"I must have passage on the ship leaving for Kingston today," I demanded, stabbing my finger in the direction of the offshore vessels.

"Well ma'am, it's completely booked," he mocked with exaggerated politeness. "Perhaps you can come back next week and try for passage."

"Try today!" I returned. "I will not overwinter in this war another year. My return to England begins today!" I slammed the Eldenmont letter on the counter, "And that ship out there will carry me!"

A British officer pushed through from behind and stood at my side. Before I had a chance to notice, he had taken up my letter from the counter.

"Charles Eldenmont! I thought as much," he muttered with disdain, returning the letter to my hand. "Pray forgive my intrusion," he mumbled, with an immediate order for the clerk to reassign his berth to us.

Speechless at his conflicting impudence and generosity, I mutely offered my hand with a curtsy of gratitude. He accepted with a curt nod of his head.

"Whom do I have the honor of thanking?" I rallied.

He looked warily at me, as if anticipating rebuke for his breech of manners. I stared back at him, baffled at the contradiction within his character. A jagged scar marred the right side of what might otherwise have been a handsome face. A beard would easily cover it. Were he inclined to smile it may have lent him roguish charm, but his face was bitter, making his noble act even more perplexing.

"Your name, sir?" I prompted.

"Captain Wesley Bryson," he answered brusquely.

"And you are acquainted with the Eldenmonts?" I dared.

"I recognized the seal," he responded, his cold benevolence persisting.

"And I recognize your kindness, sir." I curtsied again. "I am in your debt. How may I return your service?"

The clerk interrupted us with a porcine snort, "We've no room for your servant."

"My chaperone will share my berth," I mustered with dignity. "In view of my urgent demand, we would not expect more."

Captain Bryson cleared his throat. "If I might ask one simple favor," he hesitated awkwardly. "Pray give Libby a message."

"Libby, you say?" I feigned familiarity and nodded. "For certain."

He seemed to struggle to find the right words. "Tell her that I have kept safe that which she has entrusted to me," he said tersely.

"Safe?" I repeated to ensure I had heard properly. The exact wording was obviously important, from his strained expression.

"Safe," he confirmed with a firm brace of his shoulders, as if divesting an unpleasant task. "She'll understand."

With an abrupt turn he disappeared through the crowd. He deserved more mind than I gave. I managed to quietly repeat "kept safe" a few times, to try to remember my commission.

Before boarding I retrieved the books I had selected for Sammy and posted them to Reverend Strachan, rector of St. James, in York, along with an explanatory note. The Reverend would be familiar with who sheltered within his parish and, as a strong abolitionist, was

known for his support of African refugees. I also
included a note for Martha Smith, telling her that
"troubled waters" had opened a new life for me in
England.

Chapter 11

The season's fine weather remained only that day. The air grew colder, the sky turned grey; yet our two-day crossing of Lake Ontario was without incident.

At Kingston, a profound chill penetrated the air. Above us, geese flew in an ever-shifting V, urging each other south with loud honks. They wanted to leave quicker than I did. A few warning snowflakes danced around us. Winter loomed and we needed to make haste to Montreal if we were to arrive in England this year.

I found lodging at the Cartwright tavern and wrote a letter to the Colonel apologizing that I had been called away to England on family business. When posting the note, I made travel enquiries and was promptly directed to the head runner of a Montreal-bound master canoe. He was a voyageur of the old breed and I asked him in his dialect if he could make room for us among his cargo of furs.

He refused. Although the shoreline was settled with Loyalists, the reach of the Saint Lawrence River between

Lake Ontario and Montreal was still disputed with the Americans, he explained. Travel in this last leg of the descent from the high country would be fast and dangerous. English ladies could not possibly keep up on such a rigorous journey, he protested.

I heard his concerns and patiently assured him that, after two years of war and months of American occupation on the frontier, he needn't worry about my endurance. I said nothing about Nanny's ability; he was our only option. We had no wagon and if we traveled by road we would be too late to sail before winter.

With me they could travel faster than without, I insisted, if provided a musket. As an excellent marksman, I could serve as a guard and free up an oarsman. He hemmed and hawed until I offered sufficient coinage to change his mind. We would leave at dawn the following morning.

Nanny protested that she needed a few days' rest. I countered with our need for haste. Freeze-up would soon be upon us. The air felt thick, foretelling a winter storm.

As we arrived the next morning, the four oarsmen were impressed when I appeared in trousers, warmly bundled in Papa's deerskin coat, and with a knitted tuque. I comfortably cushioned Nanny among woolen blankets and we set out. The men rowed in silence to avoid detection; not singing as they usually do. Only the steady rhythm of paddles breaking water marked our presence. Both sides of the rivers had settlers, yet our rapid passage was hardly noticed. Not once were we fired upon, though it probably helped that we hugged the northern Canadian shore.

And I proved my value.

That first night I shot a deer while they set up camp. Roasted venison was a welcome addition to their usual fare of salt pork and beans. The game compensated their extra work to portage our trunks around the many rapids.

Fluent in the *Canadienne* dialect of the crew, I knew some of their songs and added my stories to theirs around the nightly inland campfire. Had I been a lad, I might have been tempted to join their crew.

I slept well under the open sky, snuggled against Nanny. Poor Nanny fared badly. Her limbs ached from cold and the cramping within a canoe. Sleeping on the hard ground added to her misery. She never complained, but was unable to suppress her subtle winces and groans.

Three days later we pulled onto the Lachine shore, just west of Montreal. I slipped a dress over my traveling clothes and hired a wagon to take us to the Grey Nuns convent, just outside the walls of Montreal. Nanny was suffering with back pain and had difficulty walking. She needed rest, yet my urgency to be rid of Canada pressed harder.

The head runner of the canoe recommended I go to the Montreal Hotel at Place D'Armes, rather than compete for passage among the many others at the harbor office. His advice proved sound. I met with a gracious British captain who had been contracted by the military to transport soldiers back to England. He made exception for the daughter of a slain missionary and provided place on his merchant vessel. We were expected to arrive in Portsmouth before late November. In three days we would depart for Quebec City, towed by a steamer.

That final journey along the inland Saint Lawrence River would take a little over a day, depending on favorable tides. At Quebec we would take on passengers from the West Indies. He assured us that, with the ship full of soldiers, we would have a door for privacy. He also extended the privilege to dine at his table with the officers. A small cabin would be partitioned for us in an inner passageway alcove between the upper and lower decks. Sale of my silver candlesticks and plate paid for board and passage. Nanny did not protest, but retreated to rest while I explored the city.

In those few remaining days in Canada I shilly-shallied between excitement and fear. The future was unknown. My dreams back in my oak up on the escarpment now seemed so limited.

Montreal tingled with life and promise. Unlike the muddy roads of York, streets were cobbled and all buildings were constructed of stone. France had banned wooden construction within its fortification to reduce danger of the city going up in flames. Shops were filled with treasures that did not make it inland to Upper Canada. Church bells chimed almost continually, impelling people to worship or at least to pause and reflect. Originally called *Ville Marie* (the City of Mary), two hundred years ago, the nearest English translation of Montreal was Royal Mountain.

From Place D'Armes I walked rue Notre-Dame to Nelson's column, looming over the public market. I bought a meat pastry and mug of ale and sat on a bench to eat by the base of the statue. This column had been recently erected in honor of the British victory at

Trafalgar. It served to remind the French colony of British power.

Amidst this crowded market near the waterfront I overheard many conversations. Within the bickering of commerce, there was a thread of talk about trade in lumber. Napoleon's War seemed to have made Canada's forests highly desirable for ship building on both sides of the Atlantic.

From the beach I searched the river for the ship that would take us to England. The current near Montreal Island was too strong for ships to anchor near shore. Passengers traveled out by *bateau*, to board. So would our small cargo of furs, castoreum, essence of spruce, and hemp grains. The Captain had said that a few civilian passengers would also be taken on in Quebec City.

Our sixty-year-old vessel, the *Albatross*, was anchored to the west, at the far end of St. Helen's Island. She had only two levels of deck, with a hull less than 200 feet in length and 50 feet in width. With her three masts furled she appeared even smaller. I wondered how she would possibly stay afloat amidst vast ocean swells and waves. The captain had assured me she was seaworthy, but he also warned that her shallow draft would make passage wet and turbulent. That did little to sooth my unease about the voyage ahead.

Looking downriver, I was startled to see a small vessel on fire, black smoke billowing up to the sky.

"Is nothing to be done about the ship that is afire?" I alerted an old sailor, who continued calmly smoking his clay pipe.

"Have you never seen a steamer, lass!" he laughed heartily, amused with my concern. "Her fire makes steam to power her paddles. No need for men to oar anymore!"

As it turned out, the vessel billowing smoke was the ship that would tow us to Quebec. I felt a sudden compulsion to visit the Sailor's Chapel of Notre-Dame-de-Bon-Secours and pray for safe passage.

From the back of the chapel I watched a nun dusting the chancel area. Gracefully, she went about her task, removing grime from the sanctified area. I waited until she finished before going forward to kneel at the railing. For centuries sailors had committed their journeys here, and I now did the same. My brief prayer consisted mostly of repeating, "Lord help me," several times. That's all I could muster before putting a coin in the offering box.

With two-days bedrest Nanny recovered sufficiently to join me for meals with the Sisters. The weather had turned much colder and a fine dust of snow now covered the ground. On our last afternoon in Montreal we bundled up and walked to Place D'Armes. A grand *fête* was underway at the Montreal Hotel and we stood among the crowd to watch a parade of extravagantly dressed men.

"It's the Gentlemen's Dining Club," a young woman gushed when I asked what the gathering was about. "It's always quite the display when they meet to direct the nation's business!"

The profusion of ruffles, gold lace, knee breeches and silver-buckled shoes on the gentlemen entering the large stone building was truly impressive. Each was lavishly dressed as if to outdo the others of their company. To my surprise, Highland Scot accents mingled with Voyageur French. The fur barons of the Beaver Club were an inclusive lot!

With passage already purchased, we were now fully committed to the journey ahead. Even if we succumbed to the tempting, secure warmth of the convent walls, our remaining funds would not last past next spring. In a clumsy attempt to lighten Nanny's concerns (and my own) I joked that if we did not sail, we would have to "take the veil" at one of the many nunneries in this lively town.

"Have you lost your faith as well as your mind, Janet?" she groaned. "You're too impulsive, like your mother."

This was the first time I'd heard her speak uncharitably of my mother. I didn't tell her about the candle I'd lit in the Sailor's Chapel. Perhaps some secrets are best kept.

Part II Away from the Oak

Chapter 12

We were grateful for the promised door.

The *Albatross* departed Montreal filled with officers in the upper deck and foot soldiers in the lower. At Quebec, an additional four gentlemen boarded before we headed into the open waters of the Gulf. Our small chamber, positioned beneath the upper and lower decks, declared us neither upper nor lower crust, but the filling in between—just like a pie. No officer or gentleman offered to exchange with our accommodation, but their small upper deck was our privilege to use for fresh air and exercise.

We were given an open invitation to dine at the captain's table. I suppose this was a privilege of being the only two women aboard ship. Only that first night after leaving Quebec City did we indulge. It was a disappointing affair.

With a discrete touch to her lips, Nanny cautioned me. I complied with difficulty and mutely listened to the gentlemen's shameless boasts of entitlement. They mocked the treaties and concessions made by the British with the indigenous, refugees and the French. Canada existed solely for their exploitation. Those who fought for the Crown existed only for their bidding and our sacrifices were the means for their prosperity.

James Cliveton was of their world. "Beauty and Booty" was not just the password used by the British navy on Lake Erie; it was their presumed right of wartime plunder.

During a lull in conversation the well-dressed gentleman at my left asked of the nature of my journey. His tanned skin, dark eyes and narrow features reminded me of a weasel. I feigned shyness and gave no reply, forcing a smile. He spoke of his recent stay in Jamaica and named people who should have impressed me. My ignorance served me well, for I knew little of what he spoke. My disinterest intrigued him. He inquired of my family and I grew uneasy. Nanny intervened, claiming fatigue, and we escaped to our humble sanctuary.

The reprieve did not last long.

Late that night we sailed into the wider reach of the Saint Lawrence Gulf and the storms of early winter began their attack. Beyond sight of land, swelling waves churned us about ferociously. Pummeled by their relentless assault we passed into the open waters of the Atlantic, where the assault escalated with cruel haphazardness.

For over 10 days we endured the terror of being lifted to mountainous heights only to be dropped into deep canyons. Heaving; swirling; rolling in this tempest; we could only pray that the next battering would not tear us apart and send us to the watery abyss beneath. The ship protested each wave with loud creaks and groans.

The shouts of men pierced through the roar of the wind as they struggled to keep us afloat. Bruised, cold and wet, we suffered this merciless torment.

Water sloshed into our berth from the passageway, soaking both bedding and clothes. The captain's boy brought our daily rations, but the food was an abomination. Cooking fires had been doused, leaving only hard weevil-peppered biscuits to eat. Drinking water was bitter, contaminated with seawater. Our slop bucket overflowed with vomit and soil and I dared not go above to empty it for fear of being washed overboard. Mercifully, the captain's boy returned to take away our waste.

Nanny took little water and even less food during this time, weakening into semi-consciousness. I lit a ship-lantern despite the risk of fire. She must not die in the dark. I held my ear to her mouth to catch her words before they could be swallowed by the howling wind.

"It was like this when we crossed to Canada," she moaned in the dim light.

"Tell me of that time, Nanny." I hoped to rally her with talk.

"Pray forgive me for what I've kept from you," she answered in a voice parched by thirst.

"What have you kept?" I stroked her face and offered her water.

She struggled to lift herself from the bunk and managed a few sips of the sour liquid.

"Open your mother's trunk." She collapsed. "Tear away the panel covering the inside hollow, behind the lock."

Was her feverish mind rambling?

I opened the trunk. The inner front was noticeably wider than the sides. Leveraging the key, I pried away a thin wooden panel behind the lock. Several folded papers were burrowed down the side.

"You were baptized as Devon Montbriar," she gasped, "and you are the daughter of Lady Catherine Montbriar." She retched with effort. "Charles Eldenmont is your mother's brother."

"My uncle?" I lay the papers on the bunk and managed a few more drops of stale water past her lips. "Don't strain so, Nanny!" I pleaded.

"Study them, Janet!" She squeezed her eyes shut. "Learn of your heritage..."

She fell back on the cot, her breath steady and shallow. Nothing more could be done except to let her rest, and so I examined the documents.

They testified to the marriages, births, baptisms and deaths of people I did not know. The Elbema Falls grave monument of my mother, Cathy Blythe, 1774–1795 agreed with the particulars of Catherine Montbriar (née Eldenmont). Nanny had also said that I was baptized Devon Montbriar. As I read the certificate a chill ran up my spine. August 3, 1792, was also my birth date. A widow, Lady Catherine and her late husband, Lord Spencer Montbriar, were named as parents. George Blythe was identified as sponsor.

Nanny awoke with a start.

"You must understand that Spencer Montbriar is your father," she rasped.

I reviewed the papers in attempt to steady my understanding. The particulars agreed with my life and an awful truth dawned. Spencer? Papa was not my father! My life was a fabrication. Everything I believed of myself was a sham that Nanny perpetuated.

I didn't want to hear about Spencer. I needed to understand why she'd raised me under such cruel deception!

"What does this mean Nanny?" I grasped her shoulders, with a firm shake.

Her eyes flew open in fear. "It means, lass, that you must live in truth. Your father was the middle son of the Earl of Montbriar, not George Blythe." She shuddered in my grip. "The eldest Philip died in the Napoleonic Wars, without an heir. William, the youngest, still lives."

"I have a grandfather still alive?" I released her.

"He'll not want any part of you, lass." She collapsed on the berth, wincing with pain. "Cathy eloped with Spencer to escape an arranged marriage—but she'd chose, far worse. Spencer was a rake, a drunkard and a gambler, and your poor, sweet mother..." Her voice cracked with emotion.

"How could you lie to me Nanny?" My anger erupted in sobs. "I thought you raised me in Christian truth!"

"I've served her all my life, lass," she said, looking up, eyes pleading for my understanding. "She wanted your best—she had so little love in her own life. She was like my own—and when her parents disowned her for refusing their choice there was nothing I could do for her. Her father let it be known she'd died of the fever.

He preferred her thought dead than known defiant," she sobbed. "Those treasures were from your grandmother; a parting gift."

My mother's tale tumbled around me. I struggled to weave the pieces together. These papers and Nanny's sincere ramblings left no doubt of two important details: my name was Devon Montbriar and George Blythe had robbed me of my birthright.

Deep sleep overcame Nanny. I had no such escape. Hours passed as I accepted the reality that those whom I trusted most had stolen my life. Had Spencer been alive he would be a viscount. Although I couldn't inherit property or peerage, I could still be his daughter, Lady Devon.

More importantly, my grandfather was alive! George Blythe and Nanny had kept me from both him and my rightful place. I was his legitimate flesh and blood, which could not be denied. I thought back to how I'd been viewed at The Forty. In that petty, prejudiced frontier I was spurned by the likes of Andrew Nettles, a farmer. And would James Cliveton have abandoned me had he known I was a "fine" lady?

His affection had been exposed as a common dalliance with a foolish girl. For that I should be grateful. I'd been preserved from greater heartache—and his rejection had roused me to act, bringing Devon Montbriar back to life.

Nanny stirred with a heartfelt groan, "Forgive me lass."

Forgive? I'd sooner forgive an enemy than her. She had squandered my trust and robbed me of my rightful place in the world.

"We did this to protect you," she repeated in pathetic justification. "Spencer abased your mother. He was weak, selfish and intent on her ruin."

"By her choices!" I answered back. "And what of this Lord Spencer?"

"His death notice is there, among the papers! Lord Montbriar was murdered two months before you were born...on his way home from a gambling...robbed of his winnings."

"How does Pa—George Blythe fit into this?"

"Your mother was left destitute and soon to give birth. Her father refused her back for he'd already claimed she'd died of the fever. The Earl did not acknowledge their marriage or your legitimacy. She had no place to go."

"The Earl?" The confusing facts danced around in my head.

"Aye, Lord Spencer's father—your grandfather—the Earl of Montbriar." She paused. "He refused to acknowledge their union as legitimate; treated her as though she was a common harlot."

"Then how does Papa fit in this sordid tale?" I again asked.

"He met her at a Mariners Mission, in London, where she organized cast-offs. The sponsor was a trusted acquaintance and knew her situation."

"And what of their marriage?"

"Your Papa was amidst preparations to leave for Upper Canada and offered her marriage. She accepted on condition that they leave the past in England. I had already left the Eldenmont household to help her in London. We had seen so much trouble that I was glad to join them in the new life."

Papa's hypocrisy pierced my heart. He had extolled marital love, yet settled for an arranged convenience. His beliefs and ideals were a fraud, just like my life.

"Then he didn't love my mother." I gritted my teeth. "So why pretend to be my father?"

"He chose to become your father, Janet, and he was your mother's friend." Nanny's voice strengthened with conviction. "That man treasured Cathy and waited until after your birth to marry so your birthright could not be challenged. As for their brief time together…love did blossom. She was truly happy and they begot a child. If not for you, he could never have borne their loss. He loved you as his own flesh."

I spat on the floor with disgust. "And he raised me like a son."

Nanny nodded slowly in appreciation. "Your mother was never strong—not like you, lass. The Canadian winter and carrying a child weakened her. Soujeesh always said she might have saved her from birth fever had she been there. And that was why your Papa felt it important that you learn healing arts. He needed you to thrive and live out all the happiness your mother hoped for you."

"Happiness?" I spat again. "I deserve better than deceit, Nanny."

"Yes, my lamb, you do." She remained steadfast to my cold anger. "Only remember your parents did what they thought best to protect you."

"From what?" My frustration deepened. I sensed she had still not told me everything.

Weakened from her effort to speak, she began to gasp. "From what you are returning to—" A fit of coughing seized her and I stroked her back until she calmed. "I've been true to your mother's dying wish." Her voiced faded and her mind began to wander. "I just don't know how Charles Eldenmont found you...perhaps your Papa wrote him."

I didn't know what was worse, the lies or the truth. Papa had shared his heart and academic knowledge without ever hinting at my rescue from London's squalor. I could have borne that truth. The more I thought about it, I accepted that I had never pursued the truth; though secrets had been alluded to, I had let them die. For that, I had to accept responsibility.

He must have loved my mother and believed he was fulfilling her wishes, but I hurt, and I was disillusioned. He was no longer my sheltering oak, rooted in my being. His favorite song had a verse that always stood out to me:

> I leaned my back against an oak,
> Thinkin' it was a trusty tree,
> But first it bent and then it broke,
> So did my love prove false to me.

Had he intentionally left this as a message for me? *First it bent and then it broke.* Whatever his failing, I believe Papa did his best for me. Love bears life out, even to the edge of human frailty.

During the night the sea calmed. I hardly cared. My heart ached; my soul unmoored. I was heading into uncharted waters. At dawn, I went out on deck to fill my lungs with the fresh air and clear my head of the peculiar numbness that now seized me.

Chapter 13

An old soldier looked up at me from the lower deck. His faded British uniform and the wooden peg that stood in place of a right leg showed his service to the Crown. I felt a kinship to the man. We were both survivors of war.

"Good day, old man!" I hollered over the din of the waves. He returned a respectful touch of his forelock.

"A kinder sea now carries us." I stepped down to the lower level to better talk with him. I needed connection and asked, "Where are you bound?"

"I've a daughter in Luton." His face crinkled into a smile of anticipation.

Little acquainted with the hamlets of England, I kept to the familiar geography of Canada.

"Were you stationed at Niagara?" I asked.

"Chateauguay," he said gruffly.

I had immediate respect for the man. Chateauguay was an ugly campaign, carried out in the swamplands of

Quebec. Disease from those fetid waters killed more than battle wounds.

"That truly was a hard victory," I acknowledged.

"Indeed," he returned. "And are you bound for home?"

The weasel of the captain's table arrested my reply. He shoved by me and brutally sent the old man to the deck.

"Away from that woman, you louse!" He roared, sliding a protective arm about my waist. The touch sent a chill up my spine.

"How dare you!" I snarled with a reflexive jab of my elbow.

He released me, dark eyes lingering as his tongue flicked over his lips. "I'm only watching out for you, with this riff-raff aboard."

I pulled my shawl tight about me. The old man dragged himself aright with his crutch. Our eyes met and he winked. The subtle gesture affirmed that I had found a comrade.

"Are these men bothering you?" Nanny stumbled down from the upper deck.

"You shouldn't be out here, Nanny." I took her arm to steady her.

"With all the flotsam about I'll not have you be alone on this deck." She turned to face the weasel. "We'll have none of your insolence with Lady Devon Montbriar!"

Both men bowed. My sordid protector offered a hand to help steady her. She glared in return and, with a quick spin, propelled me back to our cabin.

"You've come to a different world, Janet. You'll stay in the hold until you understand your place."

"What place?" I challenged.

Her glare turned on me. Her fight was back, and with calmer seas Nanny's appetite and health returned, as well. Her confession wrought a kind of freedom that seemed to strengthen her. With the burden lifted and her newfound sea legs, she took over serving duties and kept me in seclusion.

"You know how to conduct yourself in a longhouse, love. Now you'll learn, likewise, for a manor house."

I had a future to prepare for, she insisted, in a world I knew little about. Nanny made excuses to the captain that I was indisposed from sea motion and restricted my dining at his table. The officers were appreciative of our few times of attendance. We did our best to dress up and I spoke little, simply serving as a table adornment. Although the food was presented on fine silver, the quality was poor. The storm had washed the chickens overboard and polluted the stores. Salt pork, potatoes and wine were the offering. I could not complain. It was a step above the porridge and salt cod fed to the soldiers below.

That horrid weasel continued to presume to be my protector. He came below frequently to enquire as to my health. Nanny stood guard and gave him no welcome. He sent down morsels from his private store of food, which we promptly returned. We remained as aloof as possible in such small confines and we busied ourselves sewing for what awaited.

From within her trunk, Nanny retrieved an old dress of my mother's and a pair of goatskin slippers that fit over my larger feet if the lacing were loosed.

"I didn't know that you'd kept such finery! It's beautiful," I exclaimed. The rich green brocade of the dress was in unspoiled condition.

"Well don't love it too much, lass. Cut it to match those lovely dresses you saw in Montreal," she ordered. "There's plenty of yardage in that skirt. If you cut well, there should also be enough for a short coat."

While sewing, Nanny addressed those gaps of my education ignored by George Blythe. Who best to understand the manners and modes of a lady of rank than one who had spent years observing them as a servant? Slowly, under her guidance, I became acquainted the rules and roles dictating female society.

I had no choice but to forgive Nanny. She was my only ally in the world and for that I set aside hurt and anger. To rebuild trust beyond this truce would be harder; reconciliation requires honesty.

George Blythe's deceit was a difficult wrestle. He chose my dead mother's wishes over my living in the truth. He had denied me a family in England. For a man of God, these seemed unpardonable.

"He meant only your good," Nanny persistently defended. "I wager your Papa—and he will be referred to as such—raised you to be a factor's wife, on the frontier. But war changed that with new people and new ways."

In the early days of British occupation, a factor was often a natural son of aristocracy and a concubine. After a brief education in England, he might be apprenticed to the fur-trade, where tenacity rather than rank ruled. His wife was usually mixed indigenous—Métis—better suited than a European for the isolated life of the bush. She also provided an important link to Natives and, sometimes, acting in her husband's absence, even as a judge.

Whatever George Blythe's motives, he had cloistered me from society, preparing me for such a life. His secrecy around my origins was curious. I could not understand why he had erased Devon Montbriar from the earth.

I knew Nanny's actions came from misguided loyalty. Though sometimes sharp-tongued, there was no place in her heart for cruelty. I would wait patiently for more of my parents' story to seep out. The dam was now breeched; love and proximity have a way of eroding defense and she was a simple woman, devoted to my care.

The sea grew rougher as we neared England, but did not return to its earlier violence. Nanny grew queasy, retreated into quiet tension and tried to finish the clothes we had made.

"Can I get you a cup of grog from the cook?" I interrupted her hemming of the green dress. "Perhaps it will calm your nerves?"

"You're far closer to the oak than you know." Her far-away expression revealed she wrestled with more than the state of the sea. "Your Papa tried to yoke your passions for good. This world has little place for his manner of view."

My passions? Her comment was unexpected. Clearly she grappled with something beyond my knowledge.

As for Papa, his homily before going to York came to mind. It haunted me, not just because it was his last, but because of the peculiar theme. He had spoken from the Bible passage that says "I am a jealous God, visiting the iniquity of the fathers upon the children unto the third and fourth generation of them that hate Me."

At that time, I was slightly offended by his attention to a "tendency of families" to choose a graven image, rather than on an individual's free act of idolatry. His interpretation of this scripture implied that God held the family line guilty for the actions of one. This disturbed me. Didn't we live under God's loving grace?

Shortly after that he left for York. While he was gone, I had to manage the complaints of several congregants about this sermon and could not defend him. This was one of the rare times where I disagreed with him. I resolved to challenge him, upon his return, to explain how a merciful God would condemn innocent children for their parents' actions.

He never had the chance.

I've heard it said that God allows good folk to sense when their end is near so they can prepare those left behind. With horrid understanding I now realized the homily had been intended for me.

"Nanny? Did Papa fear I would take up Spencer Montbriar's indulgences?" I prompted with awakening insight. "Tell me truthfully…did he believe that I might repeat my mother's impropriety?"

She looked up, eyes widened with shock, and quietly said, "The Good Lord wants to help us get free from the family's ways, but He leaves it to us to walk it out."

Amos had left sound advice with me at Burlington Heights. *Wisdom comes when we accept that life is not simple.* Papa had not quenched my passionate nature. Instead he had fed me good things such as learning, adventure and responsibility. He had done his best to prepare me, should iniquity revisit.

On the eve of our arrival in England, I still ached from Papa's betrayal. With no idea of what lay ahead, I needed peace. Had I not forced the revelation of my birth, I wondered if I ever would have learned that Papa was not my father. I needed to press for resolution before we left the ship, so asked Nanny when she had intended to reveal the truth of my birth.

She sighed deeply, "Never, if the choice were mine."

"Then I thank God it was taken from you."

She looked at me tenderly, overlooking my rebuke. "There's more I've buried. I'm not sure if you'll be so thankful after I tell you."

"My mother eloped with a drunkard and came to ruin. I am thought to be a bastard." I leaned back on the bunk relieved that she was finally coming clean. "What more disgrace is possible, Nanny?"

"The Eldenmont fortune was built through the sugar trade," she calmly said.

My breath caught as if I had been kicked in the stomach.

"The sugar trade," I repeated to ensure I had heard her clearly.

"Aye," she confirmed with a firm nod.

My stomach roiled with revulsion. Trade in sugar was completely dependent on slavery. The Eldenmont wealth was built through countless stolen lives, families torn apart, people brutalized and killed. To live on the avails of such suffering was despicable.

"The Eldenmonts own slaves?" I tendered.

"They never kept any in England," she discreetly affirmed. "They reduced their visible holdings as they moved up in society. Marriage to Lady Charlotte had much to do with that."

Nanny then described the campaign of the Eldenmonts, in successive generations, to marry up in society and distance themselves from the sordid origin of their fortune. My uncle Charles had made a favorable union with the daughter of an impoverished earl. The intent had been for my mother to be similarly bartered in another favorable respectable union. An ancient family had been lured with sufficient dowry to shore up their estate. My mother chose to run off with Spencer, instead.

"Then you've kept in touch with my family?"

"Your Papa did, but he told me little. Perhaps he wanted you to return to England someday."

Whatever his motives, no hope existed to escape the sins of my fathers. I was about to become dependent on them, and bitter was the taste in my mouth.

Chapter 14

It was mid-November when we walked down the gangplank at Portsmouth. Two months had passed since leaving Niagara; it seemed a lifetime.

My feet were unsteady on solid ground. Months of being buffeted about could not easily be shed. Nanny was no better. Arm in arm we slowly walked along the pier to where our trunks had been deposited. An ancient castle keep overlooked the inner harbor. I thought of the prisoners of the Napoleonic war held there. Frigid Channel winds continued to find us. My newly sewn green dress, coat and bonnet kept me fashionably warm.

Soldiers from the lower decks clamored down the gangplank, merging onto the crowded pier. Men loitered hungrily about, hoping for porter work. Several prostitutes sauntered among the rabble, brazenly flaunting their sad wares. Even with pockmarked skin, and stinking of rum and vomit, they attracted interest from disembarking soldiers.

Off to my right, I recognized the old soldier from the ship. Though our acquaintance had been brief, he was one final attachment with a world left behind. I nodded discreetly in his direction and he returned a polite doff of the hat.

"We have to get away from the waterfront, Lady Devon." Nanny urged me through the throng. "Then we'll find ourselves lodging."

We had agreed it would be best if I were now called "Devon" since Uncle Charles knew me by that name.

"I'll get a porter," I offered. Our trunks waited nearby.

"Not from this lot," she barked. "They'll sooner steal our baggage. Sit on the trunks, talk to no one and avoid lingering eyes." Off she scurried, away from the waterfront, towards what she hoped were shipping offices.

I did as directed, continuing to watch the various encounters. The weasel strolled along the waterfront, far to my left, in search of someone. He turned and our eyes met. He nodded and took a few steps towards me. Fortunately, a tall man intercepted. His fashionable clothes and proud bearing set him apart in this dingy crowd. So did his prominent teeth.

From their exchange of backslapping and hand shaking, they seemed well acquainted. They continued to converse and, independently, both glanced in my direction. This new gentleman tipped his curly-brimmed high hat at me and flashed those teeth in suggestion of a smile.

I looked away, regretting that I had not heeded Nanny's caution. I hoped to have seen the last of that weasel. It now appeared that I had not only retained his interest, but had gained that of his loathsome companion.

Nanny was nowhere to be seen. That old soldier with the peg leg was nearby. I discreetly waved him over. It was a cheeky move. The old man certainly could not defend me, but I hoped he might provide distraction should that weasel continue his attention.

"Old man, how are you called?"

"Peter Cooper, milady—er—Lady Montbriar."

I was surprised that he remembered my name. In retrospect, I shouldn't have been, for I had likely been the subject of talk among bored passengers.

"How shall you travel to—er—Lupon?" From the corner of my eye I could see that the two gentlemen now paused to watch us.

"Luton, you mean?" He shrugged his shoulders with a nod towards those same men. "However the Good Lord provides. And I am at your service, milady, for I see you have garnered attention."

"Aye, and undesired as you well know," I returned. "By invoking the Good Lord, I take you to be sober and God-fearing?"

"No more than some, no worse than others. But you've only my word for that."

"And on that, I accept your offer," I paused, unsure of how to ask about his capacity for work. "Can you—"

"I can find a means and will deal with your trunks." He opened his coat, revealing the dagger on his belt, then glanced back at the men. "I know of a fine inn in the market town of Petersfield, away from this mire."

They continued to watch as Peter Cooper hailed a cart and oversaw the loading of our trunks.

"Whatever are you doing, Lady Devon?" Nanny pushed by my stalkers and, with an agitated shake of her fist, demanded that Peter immediately stop.

"Calm yourself woman," I exclaimed with haughty indignation. "I've hired the man. We're off to decent quarters just north of here."

"Peter Cooper's my name, ma'am," and with a touch to his forelock he bowed to Nanny.

"From the ship—aye—I remember you." With a sniff, she turned to me, "Once cleaned up, he'll do." She turned and shook her finger at Peter. "Mind you, we've no money to pay, but you'll have food and board for the journey north."

He chuckled with a good-natured wag of his head and offered his hand to help her onto the bench at the front of the cart. She frowned at me before accepting. After helping me up, Peter gave directions to the driver and stationed himself at the back, to guard our luggage.

Petersfield was three hours inland from Portsmouth. We rested at the Running Hart Inn. The air was fresh, the food wholesome and our beds free of vermin.

With good-natured amusement, Peter took on the role of our servant. He insisted on paying for his own lodging and only joined us for meals. From his discrete conversation I was able to glean that he was a widower with a married daughter, his only child. Out of economic necessity he had gone off to war, leaving his young daughter in the care of his brother. With his remitted pay a plot of land had been purchased near Luton, where she now lived with her husband, a blacksmith. During his time in Canada, Peter had speculated in the fur trade and amassed a small sum with intentions to farm in Canada. Losing his leg at Chateauguay ended that hope and he returned to England to finish out his years.

Upon arrival at the inn, I wrote my uncle Charles informing him of our landing in England. I gave "circumstances of war" as the reason for not earlier answering his letter.

During the wait, I explored the town and discovered a neglected physic garden off High Street. An aged descendant of the original planter was the caretaker. He was without successor and feared his garden would not survive beyond his life. In those few days I gained knowledge of healing herbs that could substitute for those I used in Canada. If I ever was fortunate to have my own garden, I would return here for cuttings and seeds to continue his healing legacy.

Within four days the Eldenmont coach arrived from Hurstmere. After the humble cart ride to Burlington Heights, canoe portage down the Saint Lawrence and our modest accommodations crossing the ocean, I would never have conceived of riding in such a majestic conveyance. Nanny's only comment was how the Eldenmonts had "come up in the world" since we had left.

The coach's deep-blue sides bore the same crest as the seal of Uncle Charles' letter. I peeked inside, admiring the upholstered benches, padded in blue velvet and furnished with thick woolen rugs. The driver managed the four docile horses from the raised front seat, while an armed groom sat at the rear. The horses rested overnight and we left early the following morning.

The journey north took nearly a full day as we skirted west of London, following toll roads. Peter Cooper sat on the rear seat with the guard. At first I thought this was out of his concern for appearance, then I realized protection was needed. The contrast of our luxury with the squalor along the way was marked. Echoes from the French revolution were still feared.

Nanny was not impressed by the ride and said she would have preferred a less conspicuous means of travel, such as a post coach.

"I fear the compromise," she sighed. "Dependency breeds complacency."

We were in no position to do anything else. After paying our accommodations our funds were becoming depleted. I was now dependent upon my uncle.

Peter Cooper left us near Watford. I was sad to say goodbye to this old warrior. His companionship had greatly eased our first few days in England. We continued along the Great North Road to Welsford, in Hertfordshire.

Chapter 15

It was late when we pulled up to the Hurstmere Gatehouse. The moon was full in the clear sky, lighting up the night. Across the road a stone church steeple stood watch over us. Beyond slept the village of Welsford.

"Have I ever been here, Nanny?" I asked.

"No, love. The old master would not have it." Nanny's stoic face contrasted her soothing voice.

With a grinding squeal, the gates opened and we continued onward. A servant raced ahead to waken the house.

Ahead, four levels of windows shimmered in that bright moonlight. The sweeping driveway towards Hurstmere House was far longer than seemed necessary. After passing through a small wood, over a narrow bridge and across a treed meadow, I began to suspect the approach had several switchbacks to create an illusion of expansive property.

The coach finally halted before the large grey stone house. Light flowed down from a large open door. A footmen was silhouetted at each side of the stone stairway.

"Much as I remember it," Nanny sniffed. "Though I'm not so familiar with this door."

One of the footmen assisted me down from the carriage. From the top of the stair a man slowly descended towards me. Mature in age, his stout physique was cloaked in a velvet coat topped with a cream cravat. This must be Charles Eldenmont.

"Uncle Charles." I curtsied and extended my hand.

"My dear niece." He took my hand and left a fluttering kiss on my cheek, but ignored Nanny.

I helped Nanny up the stairs into the house. We entered a spacious foyer with two massive golden doors flanking a grand staircase that led to the second floor.

My uncle explained that the family had retired for the night, but he offered us refreshment. I declined and he bid me goodnight. A servant led us up that grand stairway to my room, at the end of a long corridor. Nanny's room was on the floor above, in the servants' corridor. Since our three trunks had been deposited in my room. I insisted she stay with me that first night.

A flickering hearth lit the spacious room. I noted the wardrobe, writing desk, several chairs and the thick, dark-blue carpet. A heavily curtained, large window alcove overlooked the rear courtyard and stables. The feather-mattress bed welcomed Nanny and me. Underneath its brocade burgundy covering were thick woolen blankets and crisp white cotton sheets.

We fell into a deep sleep and did not awaken until mid-morning. A tray of tea and scones had been left on a serving table, just inside our door.

After breakfast, we dressed and Nanny moved her clothes up to her room. I went downstairs. The same footman who had showed us to our rooms the previous night greeted me at the bottom of the stairs. Both golden doors were now open. Each led to separate wings of the house.

"Lady Charlotte Eldenmont and Lady Olivia Fairworth are in the Morning Room," he greeted me, with a deep formal bow. I followed him through the door on the left, down a wide hallway and stepped into the bright room.

Sunlight poured in from two sides of the house. The décor made me think of a clear swimming pond. The walls were pale blue, with matching blue brocade upholstery and a plush blue carpet covered the entire floor. Two women sat at a desk—neither appeared the type to swim.

They were occupied with correspondence; one dictating, the other scribing. The older of the two women looked up and stopped dictating as I entered the room. Her grey hair was coifed high and a cream-linen dress of brightly embroidered flowers hung like a tent over her plump body. The younger scribe set down her pen. Her dark-blue wool dress accentuated her sallow complexion and gaunt physique. On such a fine day, the poor woman should be out in those gardens obtaining sun and exercise.

Both stood and the elder, my presumed aunt, approached with open arms. Though her manner attempted welcome, her terse smile revealed a foundation of irritation.

"I finally get to meet my dear niece!" She gathered me within her ample arms and a strong, flowery scent surrounded me.

"Dear Aunt Charlotte," I curtsied, upon release. "Thank you for inviting me into your home."

My uncle would be away until mid-day, she explained. He was inspecting a horse on a nearby estate, and my cousins, Daphnia and Abigail, had left for Hatfield to select dress material. The pale woman was introduced as her younger sister, Lady Olivia Fairworth. She appeared to be about thirty years of age, which seemed a rather large gap between sisters.

"We are preparing for a hunting party," my aunt stated with noticeable pride.

I should have been more astute and returned appropriate awe. My mind filled with images of hunting parties in Niagara, skinning and butchering deer carcasses. The hunting parties I was used to could be gruesome events. These ladies were not likely to bloody their hands and fine clothes at such a task.

"That sounds like a lively occasion," I attempted.

She looked at me with a sharp sniff and a quick smile. Immediately, I was conscious of both my hair and skin. I had made effort at my toilette, before coming down; still, I fell far below her standard. Personal hygiene had always been important to me, but never had I smelled so enticing.

"Is there something that you need to help settle in?" she asked.

"I need to freshen myself, dear aunt. Perhaps, might I trouble you for water and soap to be sent to my room," I answered. "I fear I still carry the odor of the ship."

She smiled in confirmation. At her bidding I took a turn about the labyrinth garden, while the bathing water was prepared. I deferred on asking Lady Olivia to join me for fresh air; perhaps in the future, when we were better acquainted.

The weather was cold, so I circled the labyrinth several times rather than risk getting entrapped in the maze. Nanny and my aunt's maid were in my room when I returned. I was surprised that a hipbath of steaming water awaited. In no time I was soaking off the grime of the past few weeks. After toweling dry, the maid tied my wet hair in rags to make curls.

"I used to do this with Lady Olivia in past years, but since—" Her hand quickly covered her mouth as if she'd revealed too much. "She has no care for her appearance," she quickly concluded.

After the maid left, Nanny reported that she had caught her rummaging through my trunk while I was outside.

"Lady Charlotte must have sent her to assess your sorry state," she said curtly.

I returned downstairs, freshly dressed, with hair tied up in curls and wrapped in a turban. The Morning Room was shadowy and deserted, the sky now overcast. Across the hall my aunt waited with my uncle, in what was called the Grand Parlor. The walls of this room were soft grey, with silver grey upholstery. I felt as if I were floating within a cloud.

Uncle Charles stood upon my entrance. He invited me to sit by his side on the settee, across from Charlotte and Olivia.

"You do look so much better," Aunt Charlotte praised.

Uncle Charles frowned in confusion, unaware of our earlier encounter.

"I was just telling dear Charlotte how regrettably my sister's situation was handled," he nodded sadly. "I'm forever thankful for George Blythe stepping up to your care."

Stepping up? I felt suddenly protective of Papa. George Blythe had done far more than that; he had taken me as his own. My uncle's intent seemed good, however, and I agreed with his expressed desire to move forward from past wrongs.

"The past belongs in the past," I concurred. "I truly appreciate your hospitality."

"We're family!" Aunt Charlotte added with an amused chuckle.

A light tea of meat tarts was placed on the low table between us. I listened to them talk of people I had never met and places I had not been. With the exception of an occasional nod to simulate interest I was free to look about and enjoy my pastry. This room was even more luxurious than the Morning Room. My fingers traced the woven design of the settee. The weave of the upholstery matched the long curtains of the room's four large windows. It was a harp motif I'd seen in a book of ancient Greek fables that I had left with Reverend Cameron. Likely he had burnt the book for being too pagan.

The delicate furniture of the room was painted light grey. I mischievously pondered whether the thin chair legs were robust enough to support the weight of my aunt. A flicker of a smile crossed the face Lady Olivia, seated across from me. For a brief instant I feared she had read my mind.

My uncle got up to put a fresh log into the fire. Turning to me, he said, "You share your mother's kindness, Devon."

"Please tell me more of my mother," I answered. "I have little memory of her."

He nodded towards the window at my back. "We were inseparable as young children and her imagination brought life to my world."

I turned to look out on the hilly meadow and imagined my mother running about. We shared a creative mind. She had this rolling pasture to inspire her and I had my oak overlooking the lake. As he spoke the words, sunlight pierced the cloud blanket stretching out shadows from edging trees. This serene landscape was far different from the wilderness where she now lay.

"That wood is where I was a Robin Hood to her Joan of Arc," he chuckled softly. "Unfortunately, after I was sent off to school we had little opportunity to play."

"More delectables?" Aunt Charlotte offered from the large tray held by the footman.

He set down the heaping plate of shortbread biscuits on a low table and my aunt again directed me to eat.

"Charles, we've talked enough! The poor girl must rest from such a long journey."

I assured her that I was not tired and then inquired when my two cousins would return from their shopping trip. They had returned earlier than expected, she said, and were in the sewing room tending to some adjustments while there was still light.

She cradled a biscuit on a linen napkin and gave it to my uncle. "Devon must be introduced to society."

"An excellent idea," he exclaimed before biting into a morsel and wiping the crumbs from his lips. "Perhaps she can be included in the Earl's hunting party—"

"I was thinking of something more appropriate to her comfort." The hard edge of her assertion could not be missed. "And she must be needing rest after such an arduous journey."

He paused to await her proposal. I also waited, wondering how she would place me both in this family and in society.

"She's come from a vicarage," she said, with a punctuating sniff. "So the cards and dancing at my brother's will be out of the question. Tea with those from the parsonage might be more appropriate. And perhaps an introduction to some suitable acquaintances."

He nodded in agreement. I had to intercede before this pronouncement became fixed.

"Dear Aunt! I am already a burden on your household, for I've come with no warning," I glanced at my uncle and received his smile. "I need no introduction to society. I only desire to be with family."

Olivia coughed and my aunt sniffed sharply. One sister seemed amused and the other vexed.

Chapter 16

I met my two cousins that evening at dinner. Nanny came to my room to help me dress. I was expected to change from clothes worn throughout the day, into evening attire. The problem was that I had little to choose from. The remade green brocade of my mother's was far too elaborate for a family meal. My serviceable grey wool dress would have to do, with a neck scarf for enhancement.

While she brushed down my dress, I asked about the large age difference between my aunt and her sister.

"I've heard that there were sons in those twelve years between," she sighed. "None survived. And with Olivia's birth, neither did their mother. Their father quickly remarried and was blessed with three boys in succession. He died eight years ago, I understand, and by law the family property passed into trusteeship and title to the eldest of their stepbrothers. The young heir now has full possession and, at age 28, Olivia is entirely dependent on her brother-in-law, Charles."

The family was seated and waiting when I entered the dining room. Lady Olivia and my aunt acknowledged me with a slight nod. I muttered an apology. Only the cousins stood to curtsey; not the Fairworth sisters; age and rank were clearly observed in this household.

Lady Olivia Fairworth had changed to a rose velvet dress, better suited to her youthful maturity and complexion. My aunt was draped in a lavender silk tent. Daphnia, the elder of my cousins, fully 19 years of age, was elegantly attired in a blue velvet dress, displaying her ample figure. Thick black hair enhanced her pale complexion and large brown eyes. The younger daughter, 17-year-old Abigail, wore a yellow linen dress that accentuated her wiry frame and thin brown hair. I surmised my green brocade would have been the more appropriate choice.

Abigail's green eyes lingered, leaving no doubt she was summing me up. Daphnia's contented gaze reminded me of my *Canadienne*, a world away, in the care of Mrs. Cameron.

Uncle Charles motioned to the single empty chair, next to Olivia. A footman pulled it out, I sat and we bowed our heads for my uncle's short blessing.

A second footman set a bowl of broth before me. Without chunks of crusty bread to soak up the liquid, I did not know how to consume the watery soup. Usually I drank thin soup like a tea. I waited to see what was expected.

Aunt Charlotte sniffed, picked up the small spoon to the right of her bowl. She skimmed the utensil across the surface, away from her, and delicately brought it to her lips. I followed her example, scooping my spoon to the outside and taking care to ensure the contents of my spoon entered my mouth silently. This meal was going to take time, for though the appearance was elegant, it was inefficient.

My cousins' fine vibrant clothing contrasted their passive manner; seen, but not heard. They made no inquiry of the circumstances of my coming to their home. Neither did they talk about their respective days or ask of how others had fared. Did they not care? Were they not in the least bit curious? Or was silence a practice of this family?

Soup bowls were replaced with plates of chicken breast and roasted root vegetables. Utensils lay around my plate in a bewildering array. Again, I observed my aunt for guidance. My uncle cleared his throat. We looked at him expectedly and he began a prolonged discourse on the virtues of a particular horse he was considering for purchase.

My thoughts drifted to my mare, confiscated by the Americans during the occupation. I wondered if she had survived. This horse seemed of similar merit.

"I would think that she would be a fine choice, Uncle," I confirmed.

"And what would you know of horse flesh?" Aunt Charlotte snapped.

"I've raced a few," I volunteered innocently. "And I had a spirited mare who seems akin."

Uncle Charles scowled as if I had offended him. Daphnia and Abigail sniggered with amusement. Olivia cast me with a sympathetic smile. I didn't know what I had done wrong—Papa and I had always discussed business over the evening meal. My appetite fled and I struggled to finish what remained on my plate.

We then adjourned to the Grand Parlor and gathered around the fireplace. My uncle read a sermon aloud. As the evening dragged, I fought off a persistent yawn under my aunt's watchful eye.

When my uncle had finished, she asked if I were proficient at the pianoforte. I answered honestly; I had never learned.

"Poor girl! You've been denied much in life. Charles, we must invite Mr. Garnett for dinner."

Daphnia groaned.

"It's only good form, my dear. Do go and practice!" Aunt Charlotte returned to study me.

"Mr. William Garnett will soon be elevated to Baronet, Devon," she sighed. "Little consolation that brings him after his wife's death only a few months ago."

"I'm truly sorry for his grief," I answered politely.

Daphnia began to play and soon we were released for the night. Nanny had taken her meal with the servants in the kitchen and waited in my room for my return. She was not surprised by my reception at the table.

"You must hold that tongue of yours, lass. You've no opinion of consequence until you marry."

"And then am I free to speak?"

"Not at all, lass. That's when you take on the thoughts and opinions of your husband."

"Then what happened with dear Aunt Charlotte?"

She snorted. "You've read that woman well!" Pulling back my bed covers, she bid me good night with a kiss.

My sleep was deep and dreamless. I awoke early, dressed and took a short walk about the grounds. The air was damp and cold, with no hint of snow. For a November morning this was much milder than Canada. I did not visit my uncle's stables, for last night's rebuke still stung. Instead I explored in the opposite direction, along the river path.

Aunt Charlotte and Uncle Charles left for Hatfield while I was out. Coffee and scones waited in the Morning Room, where my cousins and Lady Olivia were busy with handiwork. The sisters were attempting to trim their mother's brown felt bonnet, but could not agree to the positioning of ribbons. Lady Olivia sat in the farthest corner, silently cross-stitching a pew cushion, ignoring their bickering. Her grey, wool dress blended in with the shadows of the room.

I did my best to amicably reflect interest. Daphnia relinquished the bonnet to her sister and began to chatter about the upcoming hunting party. It seemed of great significance to her. I gleaned that it was to be hosted by the young Earl of Albyne, who was their uncle Nicolas Fairworth, and Olivia and Aunt Charlotte's younger half-brother.

The young earl had recently married an heiress, Elspeth Pinney, whose family held investments in shipping, mining and land holdings in the West Indies. She brought an endowment to the marriage that now freed him to move in society in a grand manner. The Eldenmont sisters were excited about meeting many fine gentlemen in his expanding society.

Abigail envied his wife, Elspeth, and her younger sister Sylvia. She had met them several times in the past few months and had found them both to be very agreeable. In addition to their wealth and poise, she praised their accomplishments and beauty.

"And...Miss Sylvia is newly engaged!" Abigail held up her mother's trimmed hat for our admiration. "Some gentlemen of her circle will be very sad."

Daphnia giggled. "We wish her the best and will do our bit to console them."

I praised her clever effort with the bonnet and asked why they did their own stitch work when they could easily afford to pay someone to do these trivial tasks. The three ladies erupted in amused twitters.

"Idle hands reflect an empty mind." Olivia mused from her far off post. She had just started a new cross-stitch pew cushion cover; a frayed cover served as her pattern. "We need to fill our days."

I soon came to appreciate her comment.

The ladies of Hurstmere spent indulged days in luxurious surroundings with very little of substance to occupy them. Although faithful in church attendance and family prayer, they did no works of charity. Instead they gossiped, ate delicacies and received a few favored ladies from neighboring estates. They did not ride those beautiful horses in the stable, nor did they enjoy those manicured garden paths except to parade through. A groundskeeper attended that teeming pond of fish at the back of the estate. I would have loved to spend mornings catching lunch but dared not risk my aunt's disapproval.

I would also have loved to lose myself in the Hurstmere library. It was an oasis of literature and scientific works, rarely touched, except when dusted by servants. Those volumes had been acquired as an investment rather than to read. The ladies restricted their interest to romantic poetry.

The early part of our day was spent either in the Morning Room or upstairs in the Sewing Room. Tedious afternoons were spent in the Grand Parlor waiting for callers. If none came, we paraded the grounds before returning to wait for our tea. After that we could go up to dress for dinner. Throughout this time my cousins prattled with envy about those whose wait was over. These were the women whose purpose had been fulfilled through a favorable marriage. My cousins envied the Pinney sisters for the successful conclusion to their wait. Lady Olivia's feelings were not so obvious.

By the end that first week I had grown bored of this pampered life and could almost sympathize with my mother's ill-considered elopement. Exploring the house and grounds lost its enticement. My body ached for physical exertion and my mind craved stimulation. In the faithful branches of my Niagara oak tree I had dreamed about living in such luxury. I now felt like a crated hen, waiting to lay an egg. Barnyard hens were even better off than I, for they could roam free and hunt grubs—they also pecked less at each other than my cousins did.

Aunt Charlotte had vigorously groomed her daughters to move up in society. She maintained control through ridicule, exclusion and by constantly shifting her favor. Daphnia and Abigail adeptly rode the ebbs and flows of faultfinding. Olivia sought to avoid it by retreating from attention and remaining elusive, yet she was often the target of her nieces' taunting. They appeared to be jealous of her, even though she was destined to live out her sister's ambition, either for social advancement or as her companion. Perhaps it was that she had arrived titled at birth, as the daughter of an earl. Unless they married well they could never hope for the same.

I reached out to my cousins, inviting their tutoring in hairstyle, scent, fashion and manners. Their condescension towards me was somewhat justified by my ignorance. I did not want to be an embarrassment to the family I now claimed.

They welcomed the diversion and enthusiastically rose to the challenge. My uncle also contributed, generously providing a small sum to address my deficiencies.

With their attention on me, Olivia gained reprieve and warmed to me. Within the confines of Charlotte's fickle favor we had become comrades.

Chapter 17

My uncle's business associate, Mr. Garnett, had agreed to come for dinner, Aunt Charlotte announced at the end of that first week. It was a welcome change to the evening ritual.

My aunt had one of Daphnia's former dresses taken in and then sent it up to me. Having worn my green brocade three times that week, I was grateful.

"She 'ad two grey silks, and this one fits a bit snug on 'er," explained the maid.

The dress was the finest I had ever worn. It fitted me loosely, but was easily taken in around the bodice. The left over material from the adjustment allowed me to make a small turban cap. Thoughtfully, my aunt had also included matching cream slippers with the gift.

Assembled in the Grand Parlor, we quietly waited for Mr. Garnett. Uncle Charles obviously wanted to impress this business associate and everyone had put effort into their appearances. While we waited for the man, Aunt Charlotte spoke of his wife's recent death, that summer.

The poor man was now left with five children between the ages of 6 months and 12 years.

The coach soon arrived with the much-anticipated guest. Mr. Garnett was a handsome man, in his mid-forties. He had a fine nose, slightly ruddy cheeks and thick black hair, graying at the temples. His older style of clothes enhanced his proud air: buttoned breeches, buckled shoes, and an open navy waistcoat, revealing a white sleeveless undercoat and matching cravat. The buttons of his undercoat pulled tightly over his paunch. I had the ugly thought that perhaps he was too cheap to spend money on a tailor or too vain to wear a corset.

I marveled at how pleasantly Daphnia greeted Mr. Garnett, given her groan upon hearing of his invitation. Abigail, too, was uncommonly agreeable, while Olivia was surprisingly cold.

Mr. Garnett extended his hand to me and inquired about my journey from Canada. I thanked him for his interest and replied that it was uneventful. He joked with Aunt Charlotte about his expectations for an excellent meal, teased Daphnia about her many suitors and concluded with an expression of delight at being "among such fine ladies".

"And how are your dear children, Mr. Garnett?" Aunt Charlotte fawned.

"I will be visiting with them over the Christmas season at my estate in Cornwall," he said with a cold smile.

My Aunt had put in much effort to impress the man. The table was set in white linen, with gleaming silverware and a previously unseen flowery porcelain dinner service. Mr. Garnett sat between my cousins, across from Olivia and me. We enjoyed several courses of fish and egg, and wine flowed freely. Uncle Charles stood at the head of the table, to carve the roast. More vegetable dishes followed before we enjoyed chocolate, fruit ices and coffee. The party grew merry, my cousins giggly and the men flushed. Mr. Garnett's eyes darted playfully between Daphnia, Olivia and myself. Too merry, I thought, for a man so recently widowed.

I found him unattractive, but no longer put much trust in my judgment of character. I had once thought James Cliveton attractive, proclaiming naively, "Handsomeness is a gift of birth. Attractiveness is a work of character." My humiliation at Burlington Heights would not soon be forgotten. Yet, this newly widowed gentleman deserved charity.

Sadly, my efforts failed. As the evening progressed my dislike deepened. I enquired of his children and received only the barest of answers. He praised only his son for a quick wittedness, and hoped that the beauty of his four daughters would improve with maturity. He then unbuttoned his undercoat, retrieved a silver toothpick from an inner pocket and began to skillfully manipulate it about his teeth. Olivia and I exchanged a look of disgust.

It was not his aging physique I found distasteful, for in living a full life we all undergo the ravage of time. Neither did his indiscreet manners repulse me—I could look the other way and ignore them—but his disinterest in his children and his self-centered presumption I could not tolerate. I went silent.

Oblivious to my feeling, he assumed my interest in whatever boring nonsense he spoke. I now appreciated how the tedious evenings of the past week had prepared me for this night. I was to be seen and not heard; like the silver candelabras that adorned the table.

We returned to the candlelight of the Grand Parlor, and another glass of port. His eyes frequently returned to me, and I had the strong impression that I was being appraised. It aggravated me so, I felt like asking if he wanted to inspect my teeth to ensure my health. The evening finally ended and Aunt Charlotte declared it a success.

The next morning, I began knitting tuques for the poor from woolen skeins I'd found in the Sewing Room. I needed to do something useful with my life. These multicolored, mismatched hats were the best I could do for now.

The last week of November was busy with making sachets of hops and lavender petals to distribute in the parish during Christmastide. I would have thought broth jellies and fruit preserves a better gift, in addition to my knitted beanies, but that choice was not up to me. Daphnia insisted this was a worthwhile undertaking because we were making them with our own hands.

Nanny was with us in the Morning Room, measuring me for a dress.

"Why are you unmarried at 22?" Olivia suddenly asked.

For a woman of 28 years, I thought her question curious.

"Aren't there more than enough officers for the ladies in Canada?" she prompted.

Abigail looked up with a broad smirk. This was the first time they had shown any interest about my life before Hurstmere. I wasn't sure what to reveal.

"Soldiers have duties to complete, Lady Olivia," Nanny quickly asserted. "Those officers face constant danger."

"Surely not!" Olivia exclaimed with surprising passion.

She must have someone that she cared for in the war, I thought. Abigail stopped stuffing her sachet, waiting for our response.

"Gentlemen do not wish to burden their loved ones at home in England," Nanny calmly responded. "Their letters spare much of the detail of living near battle. And Canadian ladies take it as their duty to provide pastimes for off—"

"Surely ladies aren't endangered!" Abigail's green eyes flashed, as if somehow we were at fault for being considered plunder. "Native savages would be barbaric, but I have complete confidence that Americans and certainly British officers would be honorable."

"The British were sometimes the worst," I flatly stated, remembering how the British military would not restrain atrocities when it served their purpose.

Nanny hissed in warning. The women of the Western Niagara did not publish the shame they endured. I was fortunate to have no such complaint. With a deep sigh I expelled resentment and returned to a temperate defense.

"Natives share what little they had. Many were refugees themselves, as are some Americans. But in living so near a battlefield there is a certain madness. An officer can spend the morning fighting for his life and that evening attend a *soirée*. Canadian ladies present themselves so as to inspire their protectors."

Nanny wrapped her measuring string around my waist. "You've blossomed since being at Hurstmere," she remarked.

That I had. Lack of exercise since leaving Canada had indeed softened my edges.

"I must know more of these ladies in the colony," Olivia insisted.

Of the Eldenmont household, she seemed my only ally. Her interest needed to be met.

"They are just like you, Olivia. Though far from England, we still care for fashion, games, food and even good wine when it can be had. We have servants and we do dress for dinner." With time, I might begin to believe the tale I wove.

"Were you part of this frontier society?" Daphnia asked, joining the inquisition.

"Not frequently, for mission work kept me busy."

"Poor you!" she purred. "We shall have to improve upon that and try to convince Mama that you should attend the party." She shot a hard look at her sister, "Won't we Abby?"

"She's not invited," Abigail pouted in protest.

"Then I will talk with my brother to ensure she is," Olivia declared in rare resistance. "I want her there."

My mind raced at the possibility of getting away from Hurstmere for a few days.

Olivia smiled sagely. "My step-brother is always interested in livening up his social circle. He's holding his party just after the feast of St. Andrew, for he wants a proper start to the Christmas season."

"How fitting," Nanny chuckled. "St. Andrew is the patron saint of unmarried women."

Olivia and I shared spontaneous laugher. Abigail punctured our camaraderie.

"Devon will be out of place," she snipped. "She hasn't the clothes, her skin is still tanned like a farm wife and her hands would shame a scullery maid."

"But she's lived through a war, Abby!" Olivia protested. "We can't hold her to such petty standards. And she will be my guest, even if we must share a bed."

"And pray help my defects," I invited. Subjection was getting easier with practice.

"Fine," Abigail retorted, smugly accepted my challenge. "Let's go to the village dressmaker immediately. The walk will do us good." She stood up, waiting for her sister's agreement.

Daphnia leapt to her feet with a dramatic wave of her hand. "Alright, I'll help get her outfitted." Dimpled cheeks framed her broad smile. "We'll see what magic is possible!"

"And I'll accompany you ladies," Nanny insisted, asserting her role as my guardian. "It's not fitting you being about without a chaperone."

The sachets were put aside and we set out on a brisk walk to the village. The Welsford shop was well stocked with hair clasps, textiles, ribbons and sweets. I bought a pair of gloves and three colorful neck scarves. The dressmaker then measured out enough materials for two dresses: one in grey wool and the other blue silk. Nanny provided my measurements and the dressmaker assured me of their delivery to Hurstmere within the week.

Chapter 18

Aunt Charlotte was quite delighted that my cousins were helping me prepare for the hunting party. In the past week, independent of her daughters, she decided I should be included in the excursion.

We gathered in the Grand Parlor and Abigail proudly described our successful trip to the village dressmaker.

"Successful hunting all around, ladies," Uncle Charles exclaimed. "Dear Devon will be introduced to society."

The grey felt bonnet on Aunt Charlotte's knee held her interest while she busily rummaged through her sewing basket.

"I agree," she finally affirmed, holding up a roll of matching ribbon. "It would be well for Devon to meet suitable gentlemen. And since she recently returned from a Canadian convent—which is what you will maintain," she said with a sharp look in my direction, "there is not much to explain. You do speak French, Devon?"

"Fluently," I answered truthfully. An old trapper and his Ojibwa wife had been my tutors. Changing the subject, I quickly offered to trim her bonnet. "I may know nothing of the latest fashion, but I am skilled with a needle."

She described how she wanted the bonnet tailored and I did as bidden.

Stir-up Sunday was the following day, and I was introduced to the Plum Pudding Ceremony. By tradition, unmarried ladies gathered in the kitchen to stir up the Christmas cake batter. We took turns at the large mixing caldron, churning in flour, eggs, suet, currents and spices. Lastly, we added silver coins and small charms to the batter. Each represented a blessing to the person who found the charm in their cake at the Christmas feast. Coins were said to bring wealth, an anchor foretold safe harbor, a thimble promised thrift, and a wishbone ensured good luck in the coming year.

When my turn came to stir, I closed my eyes and made my wish. I thought of Papa, and the hopes he had for me, and I wished for a year of dreams fulfilled. Life at Hurstmere was not what I had imagined in my old oak at Elbema Falls.

We left the batter with the cook, who would bake it into a large cake and let it marinate in brandy through the Advent season. It would be a delightful addition to the Christmas Feast.

A dancing tutor came mid-week to instruct us on the latest dances in preparation for the party. Then we were dismissed to select our clothes for the many changes throughout the day. Fortunately, my new dresses arrived earlier than promised. I quickly stitched up a muslin day dress, along with two blouses, from leftover textiles found in the sewing room.

On the eve of our departure, Nanny again reviewed and repacked my clothes.

"You've pulled together a fine assembly," she said, holding up one of the underblouses. "Clever work, lass!"

"You've taught me well, Nanny."

"Aye. Your Papa thought it was a waste. He would have preferred you work on Latin conjugations or whatnot." She refolded my blouse and returned it to the trunk. "You are more than capable of both."

"I wish you were coming Nanny," I confessed. "I'm afraid I'll do something foolish."

"I need to keep up on the servants' talk while you're away," she teased, then wiped her eye with a corner of her apron. "Do not doubt yourself, lassie. You managed to please Soujeesh, and that's as hard a task as any."

She gestured me to sit with her on the bed and took my hand. "You were raised with far more freedom than the ladies you'll be with. Mind you keep the stays on your corset tight," she wagged her finger at me. "I know the restriction is not easy."

"My family is enough of a corset for me. I can barely move."

"Well corset your speech, at least," Nanny glanced at my trunk, "and stay out of trouble."

"My clothes are so much more than I could have hoped for back home."

"This is your home now," she corrected. "Mind your uncle. I don't believe that he agreed with your mother's arranged marriage, but he did nothing on her behalf, either."

"Will he allow his daughters to marry for love?"

She chuckled and shook her head in amusement. "These people don't marry for love. They marry to build lineage and property, and your cousins will do the duty they've been bred for. That's what this gathering is all about, lass. And poor Lady Olivia…Well she has only lineage to bargain with and has put off her duty far too long."

"Won't Uncle Charles provide a settlement for her?"

"She's lived off him long enough."

That might be said of me, someday, I thought. "Why doesn't her step-brother, Nicolas, help?"

"He's a spendthrift. Take a good look around while you're there. Though the house is grand, I've heard that gentleman is up to his nose in debt. That Pinney money was sorely needed, so you must not feed your cousins with silly ideas about officers in Canada, now. These families set their sights high. A spare son may be your lot, but with their generous dowries they are expected to attract far better."

"Won't they inherit Hurstmere?"

"They'll only be given a dowry, for it is the rare lady who has her own wealth. I've been told that a distant cousin, Daniel Fremont, will inherit."

"And is he too distant to wed one of them?"

She shook her head again and I could not tell if she was amused or irritated. "Hold that tongue and spare yourself embarrassment. You are every bit a lady—so act it!"

The next morning, we set out in the Eldenmont coach. Traveling west, we stopped for a midday respite at an inn near Berkhamstead. We then continued north, through the rolling hills of Buckinghamshire, to Albyne Abbey. The Earl's estate came into the family from repossessed monastery lands during the Tudor Reformation.

The coach pulled through the entrance gates and we rode the long straight approach up to the great house. Stars twinkled in the cold, clear sky. The silhouetted minarets were visible on the roof, while four levels of paned windows shimmered with reflected light from the full moon.

Through the open door of the main entrance, the Earl stepped out. He was stylishly dressed in a tapered red coat, navy trousers and a flowing white cravat, with a footman at his side. He greeted us warmly, kissing Charlotte and Olivia on the cheek and leading them, arms linked, up to the house. Uncle Charles led his girls behind the Earl, while I trailed.

The house was far more imposing than Hurstmere. Dark wood panels lined the walls, carved with images of bears, roses and other icons of nature. Thick crimson carpeting blanketed the wooden floor, while the high ceiling disappeared into darkness. A majestic staircase, led up to an arched overlooking mezzanine. I wondered if Olivia and Charlotte found it difficult to return to their family home, now governed by another.

Lord Nicolas informed us that Lady Elspeth had only just left for a night of feasting and dance at a neighboring estate. He even offered to make arrangements for us to join them, if we wanted. Aunt Charlotte declined.

"You'll not miss out dear sister," he assured her. "I've provided a full week of activities."

"As I knew you would, Nicky," Aunt Charlotte patted his arm.

We followed him through a large open doorway to our left, into the dining room. An assortment of meats, breads and wines waited on the sideboard.

"Ah! *La petite demoiselle de Canada*," the Earl winked at me; I took immediate dislike to the man. "Charlotte wrote about you. Pray rest up for tomorrow. A good many gentlemen will join us in the hunt." He laughed at his intended slip of tongue, then added, "I mean the shoot."

I felt like a piglet fattened for market.

"Daniel Fremont has joined the party," Olivia whispered as we ascended the grand stair to our rooms.

"Oh dear! If it is a hunting party, then who is the prey?" My candor prompted a rare chuckle from her.

"It's not easy being prey," she sighed deeply. "You'll soon see."

Daphnia and Lady Olivia had their own rooms; Abigail and I shared. I surveyed our richly decorated chamber, remembering Andrew Nettles' sturdy stone cottage at The Forty. This was a far different perspective of what I once thought grand. Plush blue carpet and cream curtains matched the upholstered furniture. The bed was covered in rose damask and strewn with plump pillows. Part of me wished that Andrew could see me now; part of me was surprised I even cared.

Sleep came as soon as my head touched the silken pillow. I awoke to a housemaid opening the curtains to let in the morning sun.

"Best enjoy the day while you can, ladies," she announced brusquely. "Today's sun won't last long." With a firm shut of the door, she was gone.

I groaned. Abby pulled our blanket to her side of the bed.

We helped each other dress and went down to breakfast in the dining room. A generous array of delicacies was arranged on the sideboard, to be eaten at our leisure. Several of the gentlemen had already left for an early morning shoot; many of the ladies were breakfasting in their rooms.

I nodded to Daphnia and Olivia, enjoying their meal at the far end of the table. My attention settled on the elegant woman waiting by the buffet. Blond curls framed her fine features and the cut of her blue silk dress complemented both her fair complexion and slender neck.

"That is Miss Sylvia Pinney, Nicolas's sister-in-law," Abigail whispered as we crossed the floor to greet her. "She's also an heiress."

Being both beautiful, and an heiress made her a prize at this gathering. I held back to observe their greeting, envying the poise of her carriage.

"Dear Sylvia," Abby curtsied in deference. "I understand we will soon have the pleasure of meeting your fiancé."

Sylvia returned a shallow dip and her face lit up. "Viscount Daversham arrived only last evening, just in time to join the dancing. We had a late night, but I expect he'll soon join me for breakfast." Her eyes fixed sharply on me and she nodded curtly. "I presume you are the cousin from Canada?"

"Devon Montbriar," I replied with a curtsey. Where I fit into this pecking order, I was not sure. Abigail did not correct my omission—to title myself seemed bluster.

Sylvia Pinney turned away and filled her cup with coffee. Dismissed, I filled my plate with eggs, sausages and bread rolls. Olivia smiled warmly when I sat with her.

Through the grand doorway another guest entered. I looked up, curious. My breath caught, jarred by the specter before me. James had walked into the room.

Chapter 19

How could such be possible? There was no mistaking this was James, he stood only twenty paces from me. My mind spun. Confused thoughts raced through fragments of memory. Captain Lord Cliveton, the prominent *D* on the seal of Sammy Smith's letter of commendation and that horrid clerk's condescending "finally free of common offerings" all came together. Half-truths, omissions and lies welled up. Had I been the only one on the Canadian frontier blind to his identity?

James crossed the room with slow deliberate steps and took Sylvia Pinney's hand. His light kiss to her cheek left no misunderstanding of their intimacy. That rare smile I had once enjoyed in Elbema Falls was now hers. They exchanged a few words, he laughed, tucked her hand protectively within the fold of his arm and she led him to us.

"Lady Olivia. Allow me to present to you my fiancé, Viscount Daversham," Sylvia proudly declared.

I stood with Olivia to curtsey. He bowed in turn to each of us. Only the flinch of his jaw betrayed recognition. His eyes flashed as he also struggled to make sense of fate.

Sylvia presented me as Lady Devon Montbriar—doubtless, her use of my title was to elevate the status of her society. She then commented that I was recently arrived from Canada and inquired if we had been acquainted in the colony.

"I think not," I answered abruptly.

"Canada is vast," he offered in alignment. "And you have just arrived in this country—er—Lady Montbriar?" His comment faltered on his lips.

"I just said that, James," Sylvia patted his arm.

"Indeed I have, Viscount Daversham." I exhaled deeply and gave my attention to Sylvia. "And I've little experience of proper English society, Miss Pinney."

A frown swept across her brow. "It is peculiar that your paths never crossed. I thought all Canadian society was acquainted." She led him away to the sideboard to prepare his breakfast plate. He did not look back.

My head swam. A sour taste filled my mouth and I felt as if about to vomit.

"Are you ill?" Olivia asked perceptively.

I grappled for breath. "I'm no longer hungry—yesterday's journey has caught up—pray excuse me," I pleaded and hurried from the hall.

My stomach roiled. I managed to mount the grand stair and slam the bedroom door before violently heaving my innards into the bedpan. Over and over I convulsed until nothing more could come. Collapsing on the bed I smothered my face in my pillow, my body quaking.

"Bloody hell!" I sobbed. "Bloody, bloody hell!"

I could have never conceived such an encounter possible. From his flinch and fluster, neither had he.

I curled up on the bed, paralyzed by conflicting emotion. The louse had toyed with my heart, left without the decency of a farewell and now flaunted his intended before me. I loathed myself for how besotted and blinded I had been with naive presumption. How could I have even thought myself of consequence to such a man? I had thought myself unique when Canada was simply his means to gain fortune. He never meant to remain with the "common".

He must be belittled and scorned as I had been. I would expose him for his true character; Sylvia Pinney needed to be warned. I leapt to my feet, pacing the floor, agitated by thoughts of useless retribution. I was only soothing my pride. Nothing could be said or done. Whatever I claimed would be seen as my folly and not his fault—only women suffer for indiscretion.

I lay on the bed defeated, drained and exhausted. Hours passed as I drifted in and out of disturbed slumber.

*****

Rough waves splashed at the icy path beneath my feet. Black clouds chased me from above, threatening to pour out their rage on me. I tried to escape the deluge, the path was too slippery. Those waves lashed at my feet and I stumbled. Far off, laughter mocked my struggle.

Voices outside my window grew louder, wrestling me to consciousness. Gentlemen were returning from their afternoon shoot. The sun had already crossed the grey, overcast sky. Daylight would soon fade and I desperately needed air before the obligatory evening dinner. Abigail had not returned—or perhaps she had and left me to my condition. I knew I could count on her silence. Her family had brought me to this event, so any indiscretion reflected on them.

I splashed water on my puffy face, trying to wash the redness from my eyes. Removing my corset would have helped greatly. Instead, I could only escape to the grounds for fresh air.

With a shawl wrapped about me, I stole down the stairs. Laughter poured from the drawing room into the foyer, masking my footsteps. Slipping through the door, I raced across the lawn, towards the wooded park. A large oak tree watched from the center of the lawn, alone, as was I. Respite within her branches was not possible. My corset hampered climbing and she was not my beloved tree, now lying on the canyon floor, in Niagara. Six more days remained to be faced and endured.

A flock of partridges fluttered up to the grey sky. Likely servants were beating them out of the bushes to give the gentlemen one final shoot. Gunshots followed. I remembered stalking deer with Sammy last winter. We had only a bow and arrow but it was an honorable duel, pitting our wits against the creature.

I followed a mulched path leading into the wood. The cultivated foliage was a far cry from my Ontario bush.

Yellowing leaves fluttered overhead with sinister rustling, my recent dream still fresh in my senses. Lifting my skirts, I sprinted ahead, whipping up a blanket of dead leaves. Breathless from the corset, I stopped to stretch my arms above so I could fill my lungs. Leaves scattered in my wake; James followed closely behind. My heart stopped.

I looked for an opening in the shrubbery, back to the house; he blocked my way.

"What game are you playing here, Janet Blythe?" His voice was cold and harsh.

"Why are you stalking me, James? Have you more lies to tell? Perhaps further humiliation to inflict?"

He stepped back and proudly squared his shoulders. "I only took what you freely offered."

"You asked me to remain true when you left Elbema Falls," I spat out. "What shite is that? You were leaving to wed another."

"We never had made any—" He stopped short. Whatever he was about to spew died and he grasped my arm firmly. "What of you, Janet—or should I say Devon? You also lied." He pulled me to his side and his breath seared my cheek. "You're no missionary's daughter, but an Eldenmont!"

"I told you what I knew. You know how gullible I am. You even challenged me for that—a lively maid should be interested in her parents, right?" I looked deep into his cold grey eyes. "But I trusted too much and you are a lying snake."

He released my arm. "I am a truthful snake," he said, his voice strangely tender.

"Spit out your story, James." His admission piqued my vulnerability. "The truth this time."

"That last day in Elbema," he took my hand in his, "I had gone to York expecting to be told of my father's passing, for he'd long been ill. Instead I learned of my older brother's death in a riding accident. I was now viscount and heir to Daversham. Everything for me had changed, my choices no longer my own to make."

I heard through his justification. He had misled me that last day with half-truths, for he knew he would have to return to England. I craved to hear his acknowledgement, without excuse. Though I couldn't expose him to the world he could at least be shamed, here, before me.

"So when you declared your hope to enjoy my hospitality in the future, you lied," I primed.

"That was indeed my hope, bu—"

"Don't waste your breath, James Cliveton! Admit you did not intend to return to me. Admit you lied."

"My God! You'd be an excellent court prosecutor." He flung his arms in the air in a gesture of surrender. "I confess, yes, I lied. I was already honorably released from service, for there was no legitimate heir from my brother. So, with my father's health deteriorating, I had to return to Daversham. I had no choice."

His confession was too easily won; and given without trace of regret. I was both insulted and defused by this admission.

"You could have chosen to tell me the truth. Did it ever occur to you to be honest with me, as a fellow being in the sight of God? Truth I can manage and would have adjusted my expectations. But you insulted me to the core when you played me falsely." I restated his confession. "You had no intention of telling me you were gone for good. Own this James, own that you misled me."

"I thought it best, Janet. Friendship was no longer possible without hope for a future. You of all people should know that an amputation must be swiftly done." He looked at me intently, eyes pleading my understanding. "Forgive me, Janet. You are one of the few who deserved to be told."

"There was no friendship, James." My chest tightened. "A friend would not lie to me nor would he betray my hospitality."

He looked away and sighed deeply. "Settling in Canada had been my hope, when prospects improved after the war. And I would have if that choice—"

I cut him off. "With Sylvia waiting here, you took amusement with me."

His silence at this accusation infuriated me.

"You're a damned liar, Viscount Daversham!" I lashed out at him. "Because your prospects will certainly improve with your inheritance."

"Janet." He lowered his voice in an attempt to calm me. "Inheriting Daversham does not improve my prospects. The estate is deeply in debt and I will have hundreds of workers and tenants to provide for. Marriage with Miss Sylvia Pinney is arranged for their benefit—not mine. She was my brother's intended. I took on their marriage arrangement because I need her endowment. I will make the most of this; I have to."

"By prostituting yourself, James? After all you fought for in Canada? Their money was made off slave labor on a Jamaican sugar plantation."

"Well you certainly aren't bothered by the avails of slavery," he stabbed back with a defiant jut of his chin. "Perhaps nab a witless peer and you might also better yourself."

I gasped in disgust. His jab was accurate; the sugar trade was the means of my current comfort.

"Pray forgive me," he gripped my hand, "that was uncalled for."

I twisted around, unable to break free. "Would I give myself in marriage, it will be only for love, not to the highest bidder." I closed my eyes to hold back my tears.

"My estate is my bride." He kept me in his grasp.

I looked up into his cold grey eyes "Then I truly pity you. You might be valiant facing death, but you're a coward at living. *Sylvia* deserves better—you both do."

His face paled, as if seeing a ghost. Suddenly I was caught up in his arms. This was no lover's embrace. His rough cheek brushed against mine, his breath flow down my neck and he held me so tightly I could scarcely breath. The air grew noticeably colder, the sky darkened and an angry wind whipped about us.

"That's what I love about you, Janet," he whispered, hoarse with emotion. "You're so infuriatingly principled."

I tore from him, and ran to the house without looking back.

Chapter 20

The party had dispersed to their rooms to dress for the evening. Abigail looked up from the dressing table with pursed lips.

"Where have you been?" she demanded, slamming her brush down. "I had a housemaid take away that nasty bedpan you left for me. I hope you're up to tonight. And remember...we must do our part to not disappoint the family."

What part? How could I disappoint when I didn't know what I was supposed to do?

"Your dress is beautiful," I answered and began arranging three peacock feathers in her hair.

The vibrant green dress she'd chosen for the evening complemented her pale skin, drawing attention to her eyes. Olivia and Daphnia joined us in their finest silk dresses. Clearly a favorable impression was important for this evening's gathering. My grey wool dress suited my mood, but I chose instead Daphnia's made-over silk dress to please Aunt Charlotte.

Olivia tucked her arm within mine as we descended to the foyer. "I'm so thankful you're here. Mother insists I give attention to my presumed."

"I didn't know that you are already engaged." I had disregarded her concerns for this gathering, consumed by James' presence. My stomach fluttered in anticipation of seeing him.

"Not if I have say in the arrangement," she sighed. "Charlotte insists the understanding finally be settled with the heir to Hurstmere."

"Daniel Fremont?"

She nodded silently as we walked through the crowded foyer. Thirty had assembled in a mixture of beautiful ladies, handsome gentlemen and mature chaperones. Aunt Charlotte drew me over to introduce me to the young Countess of Albyne and Mrs. Pinney. Sylvia's mother was an older, harder version of her beautiful daughter. I found pleasure in knowing James' business arrangement would come at a cost he had not foreseen.

I looked about. He was in deep discussion with an older gentleman, near the closed doors of the Grand Hall. I felt a tug on my arm and turned to face Mr. William Garnett.

"I've been concerned for you all day, dear Devon. Abigail reported that you were indisposed." He smiled tentatively.

I had not known he was invited to this shoot. In this inhospitable room, his concerned presence was welcome.

"Thank you," I mustered sincerely. "I am quite restored. I just needed rest."

He nodded soberly, "And I am quite relieved."

A gong sounded and the large oak doors opened, beneath the grand stair. I had not yet seen this room. Nicolas motioned us in, insisting the ladies come in independently rather than be taken in.

"Let your dinner companion be a surprise," he said, directing us to search for our name card placed around the table.

No expense had been spared. The room was outfitted with a grandeur that promised a magical evening. China, silverware and candelabras gleamed in the flickering candlelight. Polished wood furnishings, crisp linens, scores of candles and the largest mirror I had ever seen enhanced the luxurious setting.

The place cards defined favor, position and status. Olivia and I were separated. She sat between two gentlemen at the far end of the table. I presumed one of them must be her intended. Charlotte was placed mid-table, flanked by her husband Charles and her brother, the earl. I joined an older vicar, Reverend Haynes and his wife, at the far end of the table. Daphnia was sat between Mr. Garnett and the Reverend.

The new Countess of Albyne had put thought into the evening's interplay. Though conversation comfortably followed around the table, I wanted none of it. The older woman next to me persisted to draw me in. Her eyes were kind, her face lined by laughter and her wit sharp.

"Pray tell me, is that Daniel Fremont seated next to Lady Olivia Fairworth?" I finally asked her. Only the proud back of the man was visible. "I've only recently returned to England and am not acquainted with the gentleman who is to inherit my uncle's estate."

"You're partially correct," Mrs. Haynes twittered. "That is Mr. Fremont—but he's no gentleman."

Her forthrightness stunned me. At that instant the man turned our way and I saw his face. My heart quickened in recognition of those prominent teeth from the Portsmouth wharf. That unpleasant waterfront companion of my stalking weasel was the heir to Hurstmere!

With sickening revulsion, I realized my uncle had tendered his titled sister-in-law to such a rake. Poor Olivia was being traded like one of his horses—to wed and bed this horrid man—all to keep property close and elevate their family in society.

Gay laughter drew my attention to Sylvia. She and James sat midway down my side of the table; the large mirror across from me gave full view of both his attentiveness and her delighted response. His every remark seemed to be met with her carefree mirth. Pathetic obsession prevented my looking away.

As the meal continued, my untouched soup was replaced with roasted partridge. The assortment of spiced vegetables might have been delicious, but I could not eat.

Mr. Garnett leaned across Daphnia. "Have you no appetite, my dear?" Daphnia frowned at me to answer him.

The heat and smell of the many candles robbed me of air. I grew light-headed, my body weak.

"Are you not well?" asked Mrs. Haynes, taking my hand gently.

"Forgive me," I offered them both, glancing back at James in the mirror's reflection. Our eyes engaged. Such a different meal this was compared to cornbread and tea around Soujeesh's welcoming fire. He looked away.

"Eat up! Eat up!" Mr. Garnett urged. "You're much too thin, Lady Devon."

"Tell me, Lord James," Daniel Fremont called out, rising to his feet to quiet the party. "Are not these lovely ladies a delicious feast after your famine in Canada?"

"Mr. Fremont, how you flatter," Sylvia fawned.

Laughter danced about the table. Olivia's widened eyes caught me with her sympathy. Mrs. Haynes squeezed my hand.

"I must disagree, Mr. Fremont," James stood up. Conversation hushed to await his reasoning. "Many fine ladies of beauty, grace and courage live in the colonies. I charge you to remember Mrs. Secord, a dear lady who saved Upper Canada from invasion."

"Who?" interrupted Nicolas's wife, Elspeth.

"Mrs. Secord. She walked twenty miles out of American-occupied territory, in the dead of night, to warn the British army of an impending attack," James returned. "I believe her heroic trek may have saved our colony."

"Alone and in the dark of night? That's not behavior fit for a lady!" Elspeth railed with shrill confidence.

"Dear Lady Elspeth," James acknowledged the comment with a bow. "If you were acquainted with Mrs. Secord, as I am, you would definitely include her with the finest of ladies. She is only one of many who captured my admiration. Another fine woman—and dear comrade—spoke the Native language fluently, fed our wounded with game she'd ably hunted, kept men from death when no surgeon could have helped, and gave refuge to all who called upon her humble home. A simple bowl of soup from her hand brought nourishment of heart, mind and body."

A flood of longing seized me. His gaze remained on Sylvia.

"A lady making soup?" she shrugged. The movement caused her shawl to slip away exposing delicate pale shoulders. "It's incredible that you returned, when such creatures abound."

"Very difficult, indeed," he returned.

"—And fortunate we are that you did," Nicolas Fairworth interrupted. "So we must toast those poor wenches you left behind." He stood, lifting his wine glass high, and pronounced, "God bless those saintly damsels!"

All gentlemen stood with shouts of "Hear, hear!"

James raised his glass to me. I felt as a moth drawn to his flame. The madness of our earlier embrace lingered. *That's what I love about you, Janet,* his words played with my heart.

"And God bless the ladies that we have here," Nicolas concluded, bowing to his wife.

James Cliveton acknowledged Sylvia with his raised glass.

Downing my glass failed to clear my mind. My weakness toward him frightened me. I needed to get away. With the main course ended, sweets were passed around. At first I politely declined, in petty protest to the sugar trade. Trying to avoid James in the mirror, I gave attention to the delicately sculpted sugar centerpiece. The seductive beauty masked its dark origin in Jamaican slavery. So did the small iced cake set before me.

"Pray eat, dear lady," Mr. Garnett again urged. "You must regain your strength."

I took a bite. The taste was pleasing. I wanted more, but returned it to my plate and placed my napkin atop.

"You're sweet enough, dear," Mrs. Haynes affirmed, noting my hesitance.

"I don't need sweets," I concurred.

"Neither do I," she laughed and bit into her cake.

The party moved to the dining room, now cleared of furniture for dancing. I longed for solitude and claimed fatigue when Mr. Garnett asked me to dance. He protested, exclaiming that he had released Daphnia to a shy Pinney nephew to better give me his full attention. I was flattered and promised to join him for a walk about the grounds the next day. I withdrew to my room. The music and merry laughter followed me up the stairs. Five days remained to endure this torment.

Chapter 21

We awoke to drenched and muddy grounds. Rain had poured down throughout the night, persisting into the dismal morning. Shooting and riding were not possible. Neither was avoiding James.

Abigail had left to breakfast. I continued my slumber, unable to eat. My stomach was still taut with strain. During the night, a calm had settled on me.

When I finally made my appearance in the early afternoon, cards were the amusement of the party, in the Salon off the dining room. I wore my grey wool dress and muslin underblouse, for I had no desire to stand out. Mrs. Haynes motioned me over to her bench in the window alcove.

"You retired last night before we could talk," she said, tenderly taking my hand as she had at dinner. "I could hardly sleep seeing your mother again. You have her eyes, you know."

"How are you acquainted with—" I floundered for words, unsure of where she was leading, "the Eldenmonts?"

"It's hard to know who to trust." She returned an understanding smile. "So I'll tell you why a humble reverend and his wife attend such a grand party." She shifted slightly, inching closer. "Young Earl Nicolas is one of our charity's benefactors. I'm of the Fairworth family—though not a close enough relation for Lady Charlotte to mind." She twittered at her self-effacement. "And we have come, at the Earl's request, to lend respectability in return for his generosity. These events always need a presence of propriety."

"You do it admirably, Mrs. Haynes." I warmed, but not enough to bite her bait.

"Agreed," she affirmed. "Now tell me of Canada."

"Aunt Charlotte has asked me not to speak of Canada… or my mother. Where are you taking me, Mrs. Haynes?"

She returned a coy wink. "Being knowledgeable is how I contribute best to my husband's work and my responsibilities as chaperone." She glanced about the room. "In the far off past, the Earl of Montbriar was a generous sponsor of our mission. Time and bitterness have long tightened his fist."

"Towards your charity?" I asked.

We both paused briefly, our eyes drawn to James standing in the doorway. He glanced about in search of someone. I returned to Mrs. Haynes.

"Now there's a fine man!" she commented off-hand, "Both Pinney sisters vied for young Nicolas, but Sylvia will end up with the far better choice, if you ask me."

She returned her attention to me. "Your grandfather was very generous until his sons—your father in particular—chose to act of their own accord." She hesitated. "Your father was an intemperate man, before he met your mother, and caused Lord Montbriar much grief. The Earl pressured us to intervene in their marriage and argue for an annulment. We refused to comply, for no man is above consequences for their deeds. That marriage was properly registered in the Scottish Church—their vows made before God." With a delicate sigh, she asked, "When will you be visiting your grandfather?"

I now assumed her intend was to use me to regain my grandfather's benevolence.

"I hardly think you can send me to intervene for your charity, dear woman. My grandfather left my mother destitute and I believe he does not even acknowledge me as legitimate spawn."

"This is not about my charity, dear. It's about your rightful place in society," she rebuked gently. "With two sons dead, and only one remaining...he may reconsider his treatment of your mother." She sighed again, which seemed to be her delicate way of redirecting conversation. "Mister Blythe—a truly good man, I might add—took your mother to Canada without presenting you to your grandfather. Your mother asked that we not reveal your whereabouts. And that was when the Earl ended his patronage of our work." She sighed again. "And how is dear Nanny?"

"Hale and hearty, although the crossing nearly brought on her end." I resisted her diversion. "Why did my mother not want him to receive me?"

"You won't discover your mother's reasoning until you speak to your grandfather. Pray write him at Waltham Abbey," she gently urged. "What harm will come of a simple note?"

"What harm?" I repeated. "I've survived enemy occupation, faced their muskets, fought hunger and murderous cold. What harm can a letter to an old man do?"

She looked ahead, quietly smiling. Breaking my word to Aunt Charlotte germinated resolve. I would write my grandfather, if only to spite Uncle Charles.

"I do see much of George Blythe in you. And be assured that your confidences are guarded. I have no living children and consider you almost as my own. Did you know that I held you only hours after your birth?"

A shadow fell on me. I looked up at James Cliveton. Oh Lord, strengthen me!

"Mrs. Haynes? Might I intrude and have a private word with Lady Devon?" he asked.

She nodded without hesitation. Perhaps my confidences were safe with her, but she had come to garner support of her husband's mission. I must never forget that. Graciously she declared a need to take a turn about the room for air, and left us.

"You appear unwell, dear Janet." He sat so close that his arm pressed against mine.

"I will mend, Viscount Daversham."

"I'm so sorry, Janet," he whispered. "I declare, with all my heart, that I would gladly go through that war again, if it meant I could be with you."

"Does taunting me relieve the boredom of your life?" I asked bluntly.

He rose to join Sylvia for a game of cards, without answering.

For the remainder of the afternoon I was forced to be near him. A proposed foxhunt had been cancelled because of the unfavorable cold. Rain had turned to sleet, icing the grounds with slush.

Chapter 22

Observing James was painfully good. The calm of my awakening remained throughout the day, heightening objectivity and quenching sentiment. I had never seen him in society and was surprised to find how differently he behaved. Absent was the man I'd jostled, sparred and raced with in Elbema Falls. This James controlled conversation with measured charm, wit and compliments.

Listening to him left me empty. He'd once said that he had no opinion save that of the Crown, and I now saw it true. Graciously he revealed nothing of himself—no thoughts or opinions—rendering his soul invisible. I almost felt sorry for him, trapped by a need to say what was expected rather than to benefit those around with tart perspective; almost.

Perhaps that shows my ignorance of society; perhaps it also reveals the depth of his character. To wonder what he'd once thought of me was not worth the bother, for it was clear that we were not suited. He was marrying for money, rather than intimacy.

With increasing acceptance of his choice, my ache lessened. I could never respect such a man.

That brief sweetness on the Niagara frontier had been a fantasy. It belonged with my old oak, now rotting on the canyon floor. Even if he had loved me, he would have eventually tired of me. In this setting, I could appreciate the deprivations of society he must have endured in Canada. Though his humiliating severance still pained me, a greater heartache had been averted. He'd spoken accurately: an amputation must be swiftly done. I had only to endure him for the remainder of this week, not for a lifetime. Likely he felt the same of me.

Mr. Garnett was nowhere to be seen. Neither was my uncle or several of the older men, including Daniel Fremont. Olivia explained that they had probably gone off somewhere to discuss business, as they usually did at such affairs. I was only glad that I did not have to fend off Mr. Garnett's attention. The promised walk could wait for another day.

By late afternoon the company was wearied by confinement. Fresh amusement was needed. Sylvia Pinney proposed that we sing. As a product of her parent's investment, her loveliness had been honed to display at a venue such as this.

"I will begin, but I must have an accompanist," she demanded with child-like impetuousness, looking about at the coquettes in the room. With a teasing stomp of her foot, she repeated the demand, this time centering out her fiancé.

"James! You must favor me as my accompanist."

He looked up at her with a dismissive shrug. "I'm a sailor, not a musician, my dear. I haven't touched an instrument since I was a child. Choose one of these lovely ladies, instead." He returned to his game of whist.

She cast her eyes about the room seeking another victim. Our eyes met and I caught her wicked glint.

"Lady Devon," she purred. "Please grace me."

My cousins must have told her that I did not play an instrument. It was no secret to the Eldenmonts that I had been cultured for work, not display. Fortunately, Soujeesh had also taught me when to wrestle and when to fake.

James Cliveton scowled and set his cards on the table. I rose to my feet, swift to deny him opportunity to come to my defense. My curtsey to Sylvia implied compliance.

"This is such a privilege, Miss Pinney," I gushed and sat down immediately. "Pray allow me no distraction from enjoying your performance. You are said to be enchanting and I wouldn't want to miss a moment."

She hesitated and I feared my praise may have been too much. Fortunately, vanity prevailed, and with a toss of her blond curls she accepted the offer of another accompanist.

Several cheery tunes about birds and flowers erupted from her. Though her melody was accurate and pleasant, it did not touch the soul. I stifled several yawns. When her repertoire finished, she joined James Cliveton, tucking her arm possessively within his. Another young lady took her place. A parade of ability soon followed, including Abigail. While none outshone Sylvia, they all tried, with an attitude not unlike the waterfront women of the Portsmouth.

Following this show, we adjourned to dress for dinner. I changed to my new dark-blue silk dress. While arranging my hair, I noted how flushed my cheeks had become. I was not ill, but enlivened as if braced for battle. A fire burned in me that I had not felt before.

We did not sit for dinner, but ate from a delicious arrangement at the sideboard. As expected, Lord Garnett sought me out, praising my appearance. I thanked him as we filled our plates to eat; his eyes lingered on me.

"Such fun!" he whispered in my ear. "I'm so pleased your appetite has returned."

A gong sounded and Aunt Charlotte nodded at me with approval. The large oaken doors opened beneath the stairway. Tonight the glittering hall had been transformed into a ballroom. Nicolas instructed the ladies to choose their partners for the first dance. Fiddlers and flutists began a set of lively dance and the ladies led their chosen gentlemen to the dance floor, in a display of flouncing and bouncing. I stood to the side, watching. At the center of the floor Sylvia laughed merrily with James Cliveton. Mr. Garnett tapped his feet, pressing me to take him to the floor.

Fortified by a quick glass of wine, I took his hand and we joined in a quadrille that I had only learned this past week. Laughingly, I followed the calls of the dance leader and we fumbled our way through. Halfway through the dance, I noticed Olivia standing alone to the side. Elspeth had chosen Daniel Fremont.

I excused myself after that first dance and joined Olivia. The next dance was for the gentlemen to choose.

"I'd rather be alone," she quickly assured me. "But I notice Mr. Garnett seems to be taken by you. Daphnia will be relieved!"

"Surely he isn't considering marriage so soon after his wife's death—and to Daphnia. She's too young."

"My father was no different." She touched my arm lightly. "Beware. Love is never kept safe with such men." She left to fetch us more wine.

James Cliveton passed by, pausing just beyond me. I half dreaded he might take me to the floor since I stood alone. He didn't and my heart sank with disappointment. Frustrated at my conflicting sentiment, I moved away, but his hand quickly grasped my arm.

"Leave me alone," I hissed.

"*Je ne t'oublierai jamais,*" he spoke so faintly I thought I only imagined it.

Never will I forget you.

"You forgot me in Canada," I whispered.

Sylvia was by his side before he could reply. She must have been watching him closely. He led her to the floor. I retired upstairs, not looking forward to another tedious day.

The *fête* continued below. Time had come for me to claim my rightful place. I found pen and letter paper and wrote my grandfather that I had returned to England and looked forward to meeting him.

Chapter 23

Iawoke with a strong compulsion to post my grandfather's letter that very day. I couldn't wait for Abigail to wake. The letter was safely stored in my boot, under the bed. Carefully I pulled the blankets back.

"I have something to tell you," she mumbled sleepily.

"About what?"

She answered with a snore. I slipped on my brown wool dress wrapped a warm shawl about me and went downstairs. The dining room was empty and a footman waited. I enquired where to post my letter, refusing his offer to take care of it. He directed me to the general store in the nearby village. Rain had stopped and the morning was frosty and cold. The two-mile hike would be just what I needed.

Halfway across the lawn, having passed under the broad oak, I heard my name called. Behind me, Olivia stumbled across the slippery grass, her bonnet untied and coat open. She carried a bundled napkin.

"I wanted to share breakfast with you," she panted, breathless from unpracticed effort.

Her delicate slippers were already wet. I offered my arm which she gladly accepted. A roll fell out of the napkin and I picked it off the ground.

"I'm walking to the village to post a letter." I bit into the roll. "You'll ruin your shoes."

"I'll gladly accompany you," she said, with an inviting smile, "And damn these shoes."

I did not presume her camaraderie and was bewildered by this latest confidence.

Once outside the gates of Albyne Abbey we followed the frost-hardened road towards the village. A farmer approached on a hay-laden wagon. I thought of poor Olivia's feet and asked if he could take us the remaining way to the village.

"Aye," he doffed his hat, "and I'll bring you back."

He refused the coin Olivia offered. I'm sure the tale he would spin of two wayward ladies from Albyne would more than compensate at the village tavern. I hoisted Olivia onto the back of the wagon and pulled myself up beside. The ride was pleasant and in no time we had arrived at the village, I had posted the letter and we stood again at the gates of Albyne.

Olivia limped across the lawn towards the manor house, without a word of complaint.

"This has done me much good," she puffed under the oak tree. "I've lived too long in the confines of other's wishes."

I didn't know how to respond to this confession.

Rain had resumed, falling on us in fat icy drops. We waited, sheltered under the oak's broad branches. I ran my fingers over the rough bark and began singing Papa's favorite song.

> I leaned my back against an oak,
> Thinkin' it was a trusty tree,
> But first it bent and then it broke,
> So did my love prove false to me.

"Your voice is beautiful," she offered, adding after a poignant pause, "too precious for here."

I leaned against this English oak. "I used to dream of living as you do," I confessed.

"I now dream of escaping it." Olivia looked ahead at the great house. "I want to learn about Canada."

"Rather than making pew cushions, eh?" I teased, trying to lighten her mood.

"Aye," she clutched my arm.

We ran out into the heavy rain, slipping on the grass, and burst into the foyer laughing. The attending footman sternly directed me to the Salon off the dining room where Aunt Charlotte waited, alone. Olivia hobbled up the stairs to her room to change from her wet clothes.

"Where have you been?" my aunt scowled, eyes burning. "Mr. Garnett is exasperated with searching high and low for you!"

With both hands, she twisted the paper in her hands before hurling it into the fire. It must have been a letter, for I heard sizzling, amidst the flames, and noted a whiff of black smoke from burning wax.

"Olivia and I went for a walk," I replied calmly.

"In this weather? In that disgusting dress?" She sniffed deeply. "Your uncle didn't spend all that money for you to be seen in rags."

"I didn't want to ruin my new clothes in this rain," I answered.

She glared at me, cheeks ruddy. "We brought you from the frontier for your betterment and have overlooked your crude manners. I've had enough of your sneaking off, instead of fulfilling obligation. Gentlemen deserve company!"

"I have failed to satisfy their needs, haven't I?" I scowled back.

"You needn't be so common," she snapped. "Even you can offer something." She pointed to the door. "Get up and change! Mr. Garnett is waiting."

With a curt nod, I left. Abigail stood at the foot of the stair, bristling with excitement.

"Have you heard the horrible news?" She continued without waiting for a response, "Viscount Daversham left last night—called away to his father's sick bed!" She clasped her hands with a squeal. "He's gone to Daversham, soon to be Earl, and Sylvia will be a countess like her sister."

It was best James Cliveton had gone. A strange stillness settled over me. He would fulfill his duty, as I'd seen him do for his men on the *Dominion*.

"Poor Lord Daversham," I summoned. "He's just lost his brother and his father nears end. These are indeed difficult times for him."

She shrugged. "Poor Sylvia! She's quite beside herself having planned for this week for so long."

I touched Abigail's arm lightly. "Let us make the most of our remaining time at Albyne Abbey, eh?" With ease I provided what was expected.

She returned to the dining room. I climbed the stairs slowly. A lump rose in my throat and tears threatened. He had said he would never forget me. How could he? In the inbred society of Britain, our paths would again cross. Goodbye would have served no purpose, but it still hurt.

You are a leader. Soujeesh's words jarred my thoughts. "Don't ever forget this, even when your people deny you a proper place."

I grasped the banister and looked over the foyer. Strength must not be wasted grieving for what never was. A storm brewed. and I needed to be ready.

Tonight I would don my blue silk dress and behave as my aunt demanded. Worrying would do nothing to make tomorrow better.

I didn't need an audience to sing.

Lady Devon Montbriar
December 1814

Book two Never Far

Chapter 1

I waited alone in the dark salon. Indentations remained in the cushions of Aunt Charlotte's chair. The fire had died down; hopefully the same was true of her anger.

She was still upstairs, changing for dinner along with others from the party. I had promptly returned from my room as ordered, primped, plumed, and slightly chilly in my blue silk dress.

I pulled a log from the carrier and knelt to build up the fire. Carefully, I placed it in the ashes, within the still shimmering coals. No need to stir up sparks; this room had been disturbed enough today. Aunt Charlotte wasn't used to being challenged.

The fire quickly took to the dry wood and flames began sending dancing light around the room. In the flickering glow my eye caught a red button off to the side, just outside the hearth. I picked it up and chuckled with a half snort. It was a flattened nugget of red sealing wax.

My frugal frontier upbringing would always be part of me. Building up the dying fire had come naturally. So had claiming a lost button. Nanny had drilled that into me with her favorite proverb: "He who does not stoop for a pin will never be worth a pound."

A lump rose in my throat. Dear Nanny was back at Hurstmere, my mother's childhood home, working as a servant. I was at this shooting party learning my place in my aunt's society.

I rolled the wax bit between my fingers about to flip it into the flames. On the underside was embossed a familiar *D*. A shiver ran through me. I recognized James Cliveton's seal from my time in Canada. Unsettled, I sat down on the settee across from the hearth.

Why was his seal here? To whom had he written?

He had left during the night to be at his dying father's bedside. "*Je ne t'oublierai jamais.*" His last words to me were part of a Voyageur song: "I have loved you for a long time. Never will I forget you."

Whatever he had written was ashes. Only this identifying lump of wax remained as witness. The seal must have come to this room only today, for the hearth was swept clean each morning.

Tears welled up. I clutched the bit in my fist, then slipped it into my pocket.

"Are you unwell?" Sylvia Pinney stepped out from the shadows and took over my aunt's vacated chair. I didn't know how long she had been watching me.

"Smoke," I choked.

In our three-day acquaintance I had exchanged few words with James' fiancé—no more than necessary.

"But you are so robust and healthy, Lady Devon." She leaned forward as if to invite confidence.

How was I to know that James would become Viscount Daversham upon death of his older brother? I didn't even know my own birth name before crossing from Canada to England. Sylvia had witnessed our unanticipated reunion three days ago, where we stoically denied any acquaintance fearing to expose what we'd once shared. She must have her suspicions. Even strangers would be expected to align vignettes and reminisces of colonial life and the war that now had ended. Neither of us dared such facade. He had returned for a marriage arranged to benefit his impoverished estate. I returned because I considered myself impoverished. Neither of us wanted our past to encroach on the future.

"I walked to the village with Lady Olivia this morning," I finally offered, "and am still feeling the effects of getting thoroughly soaked."

Her shawl slipped from her pale shoulders. I looked away at the fire. *Handsomeness is a gift of birth, attractiveness a work of character*. James and I had laughed in those far off Canadian days, at his confessed need of more work. I had not heard him laugh freely in the three days we shared here.

"We actually rode part of the way on a farmer's hay wagon," I added, wanting to provoke the woman.

A frown flitted across her face. "How easily you seduced Lady Olivia to indelicate behavior," her lips curled teasingly.

She wasn't worth a comeback. Having James bound to such a shrew, was all the pleasure I needed.

"Did you enjoy similar escapades with the Viscount in Canada?"

I was stung and unable to reply.

"How could that be possible, Sylvia?" Mrs. Haynes slipped in quietly and sat next to me on the settee. "Lady Devon spent the war cloistered at her stepfather's mission. I believe the Viscount was serving in the Royal Navy." She took my hand.

I studied the vine-themed design of the plush carpet at my feet. Intertwined in the foliage a silken serpent watched me. So did Sylvia.

"I do hope the Earl soon returns to health." I looked up: our eyes locked. "It would be good to begin your marriage without the heavy responsibility of Daversham."

"He has taken a turn and will not long be with us." She pursed her lips. "I had hoped to travel north to assist Viscount Daversham, but thought it best he settle these matters alone."

My fists clenched. Two days ago he had taken me in his arms, declaring his marriage to Sylvia would be out of duty. I had called him a coward for keeping this from me in Canada. His betrayal I would never forget. Neither would I forget how we whooped and hollered, urging our horses on, up the escarpment and across the warrior's meadow to the Mohawk village. Briefly we had escaped war on that sunny day, surrendering to desire I thought genuine. Only months later, when posting a letter to him, had I learned of his departure for England to marry this woman.

"I'm not one to gossip," I said, clearing my throat. Sylvia again leaned forward. "There was talk of a naval captain who was quite popular among the Niagara ladies."

"Gentlemen will have their dalliances," she sniffed sharply, "which we must never take seriously."

"Of course, when they have nothing—" I felt the pressure of Mrs. Haynes hand and stopped. Stirring Sylvia's ire would not help my situation with Aunt Charlotte. They were related through marriage. "When they have nothing to compare with those at home." I quickly substituted. "A young sailor treated at our mission did sail under Captain Cliveton and declared himself fortunate to have served under such a 'fine man'."

Fine man? Mathew had been left at the Elbema Falls mission to die. Soujeesh had amputated his badly mangled leg, while I had nursed him back to life and James had written a glowing commendation for a favorable land grant that he now farmed. He had written the same for young Sammy Smith in appreciation for fetching Soujeesh from the Mohawk village. Nothing had been left for me, not even a decent farewell. I reached into my pocket, touching the lump of wax.

Sylvia stood up and readjusted her shawl. "I am expected to help my sister plan a game of charades for tonight's amusement."

We did not get up at her departure. I exhaled deeply.

Mrs. Haynes turned to me and immediately inquired of

my interest in Mr. William Garnett. Her forthrightness surprised me. She was the sole person I could trust at this market of money, influence and romance. Her role extended beyond keeping ladies and gentlemen respectably apart, to gleaning information regarding the profitability of encouraging such alliances.

"If you are acting as chaperon I will acknowledge he is handsome and well kept for a man in his mid-forties," I answered coyly. "And I am fulfilling my social obligations to my aunt."

"I ask as a friend, my dear. He is quite wealthy and is favored to soon be elevated to Sir William for his financial contribution to the war effort. And I am—"

"Tell me what you know of my uncle's business dealings with the man," I interrupted.

"Neither are abolitionists." She nodded sagely. "Both have prospered from slavery through their dealings in sugar, rum and tobacco."

"And I am being offered as barter, even with my lineage?"

"He's not buying a horse, Devon. A penniless dependent is still an asset, if she brings family connections. You are a Montbriar and your grandfather is an earl. Acquiring you will further elevate Mr. Garnett's status and give your uncle influence in the House of Lords."

"I've written my grandfather and walked to the village to post it myself," I hastily offered, knowing our privacy would soon end.

"Wise move, my dear! One never knows who to trust at these affairs," she sighed. "The Reverend has fared quite well at this party, soliciting several financial commitments for our Mission. Guilt quickens generosity." Her shrewd gaze returned to me. "Mr. Garnett liked what he saw last month when dining at the Eldenmonts."

"I loathe the man," I returned. "His wife lies warm in her grave. He should hire a nanny for his children and find a mistress."

"I am relieved. I feared you might give way to Lady Charlotte's persuasion. I consider you like a daughter."

"Until returning to England, I thought of myself as Jane Blythe, the vicar's daughter."

"George Blythe was a good man." She squeezed my hand. "You were fortunate that he took you as his own. Spencer Montbriar had no sense of morality and preyed upon whomever he fancied. It was at an event much like this that he seduced your mother. She was intended for his older brother, you know."

I got to my feet, stunned by the disclosure. Slowly I circled the settee, unable to sit. "My poor trusting mother," I whispered.

Mrs. Haynes winced in sympathy. "He trounced her off to Scotland and though they returned legally wed, both families disowned them for ruining their plans." She glanced back at the empty doorway. "Women are always held to account," she whispered. "Had your mother lived, you would be safely nested in Canada, far from these schemes."

"We would still have to return to England, Mrs. Haynes. With Papa's murder, the Mission Board took back the clergy reserve, leaving Nanny and I without home or pension. It was either be a governess or find someone to marry. Woman's role in the Church is limited to serving her husband. What hope do we offer when faithful Christian women are treated so shabbily?"

Mrs. Haynes went ashen.

"Pray forgive me," I hastened, sitting again beside her. "I am far too outspoken and didn't mean to insult the work of your mission—"

"It is not my mission, but my husband's," she faltered. "If he should die I would be out on the streets, no different from those mariner's wives I claim to help, for I have no children to take me in my old age."

"Then, should I have a roof someday, you are welcome to share it."

"I think we would do well together." She took my hand and smiled softly. "Have you left any broken hearts in Canada?"

The nugget of wax weighted heavy in my pocket.

"I once had an understanding with a Loyalist farmer, Andrew Nettles," I provided in a semblance of confidence. "But, with the war, thought it best to not continue. He's now happily wed to a better-suited companion."

We stood to leave. I turned and tossed the lump of wax into the flames.